Stefan Cvetl

# Songs & Legends
# of
# Kraljević Marko

The World Tree
stefancvetkovic12@gmail.com

# Preface

Serbian and South Slavic epic poetry contain many mythological motifs which stem from our primordial past, and can be compared to the rich mythology of Europe preserved through the centuries. Over time not a lot of interpretations have been proposed by academic scholars, and many of those that were proposed simply failed to recognize the depth and complexity of the songs. On the other hand, some of them did recognize an evolution of a pattern through time, and proposed excellent interpretations, but never managed to find all the puzzle pieces and complete the whole picture. This is why I used some of their results, and combined them with my knowledge and understanding of mythology, in order to present a clearer image of the meaning behind these songs and legends. They represented the core of the spiritual and cultural life of people, and as such they accumulated various historical and religious layers, yet their essence remained the same. We will see how these layers came to existence, as the historical circumstances changed, and once we have understood them, the purpose of the songs will become obvious. Marko Kraljević is just a layer, who was a real historical person from the XVth century, although in the epic songs he inherited many aspects from his pagan predecessors, therefore a distinction should be made between the historical character and the mythological one. By examining the songs and comparing them with other myths and folklore accounts, we will discover who he really was, and what his adventures represented.

As such, the book is not a mere collection of songs and legends, but a study of their history, symbols and meaning, in order to present them in such a way that they have never been before. More importantly, the book is meant to honour our ancestors by preserving their knowledge for the generations to come. By doing so, we participate in something greater than ourselves, leave a mark in eternity, a trace which will one day lead us back to ourselves again.

# Marko Kraljević
## History

During the XIVth century the Serbian Empire reached its peak, and naturally after the peak begins the gradual fall, which in this case resulted in the Ottoman reign over the Balkans. During this time the Serbian Empire was ruled by Tsar Stefan Uroš IV Dušan, known as Dušan the Mighty, becoming one of the most powerful monarchs of the century. During his rule Serbia was a great power in the Balkans, its territory stretching from the Danube in the north to the Gulf of Corynth in the south, with its capital in Skopje, capital of modern day North Macedonia. After his death in 1355, his nineteen year old son Stefan Uroš V, known as Uroš the Weak, inherited the role of Emperor until his death in 1371. During his rule the Serbian Empire gradually lost its power, and many Serbian noblemen became independent from the central governance of the Empire, hence the nickname Uroš the Weak. King Vukašin (V'lkašin) Mrnjavčević was the co-ruler of Tsar Stefan Uroš V, and the father of the brothers Marko, Andrijaš, Dmitar and Ivaniš Mrnjavčević. In late 1370 or early 1371 Vukašin crowned his son Marko „Young King", meaning that he would become the successor of Uroš since Uroš was childless. After the death of Vukašin, his father in the battle of Maritsa, on 26th September 1371 against the Ottoman Empire, Marko became a king and thus co-ruler of Tsar Stefan Uroš V. Shortly after, in early December of 1371 Tsar Stefan Uroš V died, making Marko the formal sovereign of Serbia. However, Serbian lords who had become independent from the central authority did not consider him as their ruler at all, and by 1377 a big portion of the land which Marko inherited from his father was taken over by some of them.

After the death of Tsar Stefan Uroš V, the most powerful ruler of nothern Serbia was Lazar Hrebeljanović, who created the largest and most powerful state on the territory of the disintegrated Serbian Empire, referred to by historians as Moravian

Serbia. He wanted to resurrect the Serbian Empire and become its ruler, for which he had the full support of the Serbian Orthodox Church, but the Serbian nobility did not recognize him as their supreme ruler, and even though he is often called Tsar in the Serbian epic poetry, he only held the title of prince. He was killed in the battle of Kosovo in June 1389, and his son and successor Stefan Lazarević accepted Ottoman suzerainty in the summer of 1390.

Marko Mrnjavčević was a king from 1371 to 1395, centered in the town of Prilep, capital of the realm governed by his father which Marko inherited after his death, in the western part of today's North Macedonia. He was born in 1335 and died in 1395 in the battle of Rovine, fighting for the Ottomans against the Wallachians. It is unknown when he became an Ottoman vassal, but it is certain that he fought in the battle on the side of the Ottomans, along with Stefan Lazarević and Konstantin Dragaš; after his death his land was annexed by the Ottomans.

Thirty-six years after the battle of Rovine, Konstantin the Philosopher wrote the *Biography of Despot Stefan Lazarević* and recorded what Marko said to Dragaš on the eve of the battle: "I pray the Lord to help the Christians, and for me to be among the first to die in this war." Marko is disliked by many because of the image which the official historiography presents of him, as an Ottoman vassal, but the reality of the situation is that Marko truly did defend his land as much as he could before becoming a vassal. He became a vassal only after all the surrounding Christian rulers became vassals, because that was the only way he could continue to govern his realm and protect the people from Ottoman attacks. And unlike his two brothers who immigrated to Hungary, Marko stayed with his people until death, which is probably one of the reasons he became such a legendary person, and not someone else who was much more important at that time. Therefore, when the songs and tales describe him as a protector of the weak and helpless, a fighter against Turkish oppression and injustice in general, we should understand that it is the true image of who he was.

# MYTH & LEGEND

Marko's sword

Marko, the most popular hero of Serbian and generally South Slavic epic poetry, from the Alps to the Black Sea, where he is called "Kraljević Marko; Kraljić Marko; Krale Marko; Krali Marko; Kral Marko" (*kraljević* means "prince" or "king's son", whereas *kral* means "king") is representing a type of role model, the essence of the spirit of the people, despite the fact that their lands were now under Ottoman rule. He appears as a good, honourable, loyal, brave and honest person, but he is also cunning and sometimes even short-tempered or cruel. South Slavic poems and legends about Kraljević Marko are mostly based on myths much older than the historical Marko Mrnjavčević, hence why we find very little historical information in them.

So we should not associate the historical person with the mythological one. They do not follow and storyline either, but what binds them together are Marko's life events and adventures, in which he is sometimes accompanied by XIVth to XVIth century heroes, such as Sibinjanin Janko (John Hunyadi), Miloš Obilić, Relja Krilatica (Hrelja Ohmućević), Vuk the Fiery Dragon (Vuk Grgurević), or Banović Sekula.

Marko's appearance in the folklore is imposing and terrifying, represented as an epic hero, riding his mythical horse and armed with a mace, a sharp damascus saber swinging at his waist, and a spear strapped across his back. It is said that Marko's mace weighed 66 okas (85kg; 187lb), and hung on the left side of his saddle, balanced by a full wineskin hanging on the right side, which he always shared with his horse. In one of the poems Marko is described as having:

> *„...Leech eyebrows,*
> *like black swallow wings.*
> *He holds a war spear in his hand,*
> *Tall as a thin aspen,*
> *He's covered himself with a hide,*
> *A cloak -*
> *He blackens as a dark cloud."*

The poems also speak of him as having „*the eyes of a falcon*", a dark mustache the size of „*a six-month-old lamb*", wearing „*a cap of wolf skin*" pulled down to his dark eyes, and a „*cloak of wolf skin*" or „*cloak of bear skin*". Keep this in mind, as it is very important in order to understand the symbolism behind Marko and his adventures.

He was obviously imagined as having immense strength, tall and terrifying, darkening the earth as a cloud of storm. A fitting image for a thunder God, wouldn't you say? In some places he was imagined as a giant whose head touched the clouds whilst he walked by stepping on hilltops. Some legends say that he helped God shape the earth, and created the river gorge in **Demir Kapija** ("Iron Gate") with a stroke of his saber. He was associated with large **boulders which** were said to be thrown by him from a hill, and depressions in stones which were said to be his footprints, the hoof prints of his horse, or his hand prints.

Some of these have a sacred meaning to the local community, as the rainwater collected in these holes was considered to have healing properties, and coins for good luck are thrown in them to this day. He was also connected with various geographic features such as hills, glens, cliffs, caves, rivers, brooks and groves, which he created or at which he did something memorable, explaining why they are usually named after him. Such toponyms exist all over the Balkan peninsula, and similar legendary stones, lakes, hilltops, caves, forests and other elements of the European landscape were firstly dedicated to the deities of yore. Later on heroes like Marko replaced them, for the myths surrounding the deities were "inscribed" in the landscapes around people, where they honoured the Gods by performing sacred rituals, in accordance with the seasonal and astronomical changes. By doing so, they maintained the living spirit of their ancestors, they were nourished by their wisdom, and inspired by their strength to be better, and overcome anything.

The enemies of Europe as a biological and spiritual term, such as the Abrahamic religions or modern day globalists, were and still are very much aware of this, which is why they still struggle to cut off our roots, so that we would more easily accept whatever they want us to believe.

One such attempt is to make us believe that our forebears understood their myths and tales in a literal way, believing that the gods were actually gigantic beings somewhere out there in the sky, watching over them. This is of course nonsense.

It's a result of a thoroughly Christian, or more precisely Abrahamic perspective on the essentially animistic traditions of our forebears. European myths and fairy tales are metaphorical. They contain symbols which hide a deeper meaning, a riddle which needs to be solved, whose answer will elevate man to his divine nature. If they are understood literally, they make no sense, as they are full of absurd and immoral scenarios. Chariots pilled by goats through the sky? Flying horses? Dragons or three headed dragons even? One has to be a fool not to understand that these are all metaphors, hiding a deeper meaning. The metaphors evolved, changed and adapted through time according to the circumstances of the people in Europe, but the context they appear in and the meaning they carry remained the same. This is why we have numerous mythologies in Europe, all seemingly different because they have separated and evolved differently, and have been recorded thousands of years apart, but still in essence they are the same: they stem from the same pre-historic root.

We can see the same happening during the medieval Ottoman period of the Balkans, where the protectors of the people – the dragon and giant slaying Gods became knights, princes and kings with abnormal abilities, like Kraljević Marko.

The metaphors changed and adapted to the time and environment the people lived in, but the context and meaning remained the same as it was when the ancient native European first began to understand the mysteries of nature, as I will show later on.

Marko's life is full of mythological metaphors, from his birth until his death his adventures are always accompanied by mythological beings. For example, the poems say that when Marko was born, king Vukašin threw him into a river in order to avoid the fate which the *Narečnici* (Fates; Norns) foretold, but the boy was saved by a cowherd who adopted him, and later on he gained his strength after a *vila* (fairy; nymph) suckled him.

In some legends, Marko's horse was also a gift from a vila, while another story says that he was looking for a horse that could bear him, and to test a horse he would grab him by the tail and sling him over his shoulder. Seeing a diseased piebald foal, Marko grabbed him by the tail but could not move him, so he bought and cured the foal, naming him *Šarac*, meaning "patterned". He grew up and became a very powerful horse and Marko's inseparable companion. Macedonian legend has it that Marko, following a vila's advice, captured a sick horse on a mountain and cured him. Crusted patches on the horse's skin grew white hairs, and he became a piebald. Marko's horse is sometimes described as having wings, he talks, drinks wine with the hero and sometimes rescues him from danger.

In some poems Marko is said to have died after 300 or 365 years of life, but in most folk accounts it is said that he did not die, he is immortal because he drank from the "immortal water", and so he just went in a cave, in a moss-covered den or in an unknown land, where he stuck his saber into a rock and fell asleep, waiting for his time to come again, when he will rid the world from all evil and injustice. According to Macedonian tradition Marko drank "eagle's water" which is the same as the "immortal water" which made him immortal, so it is said that he is with St. Elijah (Ilya) in heaven.

Kuzman Šapkarev in his „Zbornik" noted that *"Marko became immortal because he drank from the immortal water, given to him by the fairies, his blood-sisters."* This water appears in various ways within the songs, most often as a lake, spring or well which the fairies keep restrained, but Marko drinks from it and defeats the fairies. However sometimes we do see its magical properties, for example in the song "The seven fairies in the Volujak mountain" a fairy kills Marko's friend Relja.

Marko captures her and threatens her that if she does not bring his friend back to life he will kill her, so she calls her fairy friends and tells them:

> „'Bring me water from the lake,
> So that I may revive Relja!'
> Brought her, the seven friends,
> Brought her water from the lake.
> She poured it on Relja,
> Thus he jumped on his legs!"

The fact that Marko is in a close relationship to St. Ilya is very interesting, because St. Ilya is the successor of the ancient Slavic sky father **Perun**, inheriting most of his attributes after the Slavs were converted to Christianity. So this Christianized legend that Marko is in heaven with Saint Ilya could possibly reflect an older myth in which the honourable heroes would become immortal and live on in the halls of their great Gods, which in this case would be Perun. This of course is just another metaphor. And although such myths are not recorded among the Slavs, at least not to my knowledge, they exist throughout all of Europe, with the most popular probably being the one of Valhalla, Odin's hall, so we should not be surprised if this was the case, as I think so.

Marko as well inherited many of Perun's attributes and appears in some poems in the role that Perun would have, as I have shown briefly in my first book "Chernobog's Riddles". Likewise, the fact that Marko is known for throwing stones from hilltops also links him to Perun, as the hilltops and mountain peaks in the mythology is always the realm of the sky/thunder god, whilst the stone is the most ancient representation of his weapon, which would later evolve to be an axe, hammer, or even arrows as attested in Slavic folklore.

Whenever farmers found Neolithic stone arrow heads they said that it's the arrow of Perun, and later of St. Ilya, which got stuck in the ground when the lightning hit, and emerged after seven years, and they kept them as lucky charms, believing that they would protect them against lightning.

Likewise when they found Neolithic stone axe heads they wore them on their belts, or put them on the roofs of houses because of the same reason. Much of these beliefs are nothing more than superstitions, because they are recorded in a post-Christian era where the understanding of the old traditions was already very much degraded.

The oldest traces of this cult can be found among the Neanderthals, who placed the stone axe/hammer (biface) on the chest of the dead, representing their heart. So when a child would participate in a reincarnation ritual, it would obtain the biface and kindle a fire with it, symbolically re-kindling his own life. Fire and blood are the same in European mythology, symbolically of course. This is why the Slavic term *voskresenie* meaning "resurrection" literally translates as "re-kindling the fire", which also explains why we find flint and steel kits in Slavic graves. Therefore, symbolically the weapon of the thunderer is the living heart i.e. the heart of the one who is successfully (re)born.

Marko's mace

But in mythology this can also be a club, like the club of Heracles, or a mace, like that of Marko, which in the Stone Age was made from a simple club, by adding sharp spikes of stones, like flint or obsidian.

Marko's mace is a Pernach type of mace, which is a flanged mace originating in the XII century, in the region of Kievan Rus', and its name is derived from the Slavic word *pero* meaning "feather". This is why in some poems Marko's mace is described as "six-feathered" (*шестопер/šestoper*), which again links us to Perun, considering that his symbol is represented as a six-petaled rosette ✲, reffered to as Perunika, Gromovit Znak („Thundermark") or Svarica, and it was drawn or carved on houses to protect them from lightning strikes, same as the stone axe and arrow heads. Interestingly, the word *pero* („feather") is etymologically related to Perun, whose name means „beater; striker", derived from the root *peru- meaning „stone", again the weapon of the thunderer, and related to *perkwu which means „oak", which explains why the oak was the tree dedicated to Perun among Slavs. The link between „hitting" and „feather" is made simply because the feathers on the wings of birds literally „hit" through the air. In Proto-Slavic the word *perunъ* means „thunder".

Another attribute of Marko which relates him to

Perun is that he was considered to be a fiery dragon. A unique element in Serbian and South Slavic folklore is that a fiery dragon (*"Ognjeni Zmaj; Ognen Zmej"*) was a person of great courage, a hero and protector of the people who earned a great reputation, such as Kraljević Marko, Vuk Grgurević, and other historical people. But dragons were also the sorcerers of the village, so to speak, and many beliefs are connected to them as well. It was said that they were born with the caul, of they were born with wings, with a tail, and so forth, and they are very similar to the Italian *Benandanti*. Their main role was to protect the village against the „water dragons", or various dragon like creatures which in South Slavic folklore can be called *aždaja*, *ala* or *lamja*, and they did this by going in a sort of trance, where their spirit would take the shape of an animal, or a dragon, and fly away to the clouds to do battle with these malevolent creatures. Creatures which were generally associated with bringing bad weather, devastating the crops, or causing drought. The opponents of these beings were, as we said the fire dragons, also known as *vetrovnjak* (from the word *vetar*, meaning "wind"), but in Slovenia also known as *kresniki*, whose name is derived from their local variation of Perun named Kresnik.

The appearance of the malevolent creatures varies from one region to another because people developed their imagination quite a lot, but in essence these three terms are synonyms for the same creature, which is why they share many characteristics. So let's examine some of the common points which they share:

**Lamja** – From the Greek word λάμια, according to one belief a Lamja is a feminine being similar to a giant lizard, with a body covered in yellow scales. It has four legs with sharp claws, a long tail, big wings, a big head with big shining eyes, a wide jaw and sharp teeth, and sometimes it can appear as an old woman. When screaming the being creates such a strong cold wind that big trees fall, hay stacks fly away, and sometimes humans as well. According to one belief from Bulgaria, a Lamja is a gigantic winged serpent like being with **three heads**, **six wings** and **nine tails**. In the Rhodope mountains we find a similar description, only here it has **nine heads**, **six wings** and **nine tails**. In some cases the Lamja spews fire from its mouth.

What all Lamjas have in common is that they are very big, not very intelligent, furious and gluttonous beings with multiple heads, most often three. They all live in caves, at the bottom of the sea or lake, or in great trees. They often cause drought by restraining the waters, and when they do that they often ask for a human sacrifice so that they would release the waters, but usually saints like Ilya, George, of the dragon men kill them. According to some they also keep vast amounts of hidden treasure in their caves.

**Ala** – From the Greek word χαλάζι, meaning "hail". In the regions of Boljevac and Samokov the Ala is described as a giant creature in the shape of a mighty black whirlwind which destroys everything in front of itself, and leaves a desert behind it. In Levač the Ala is described as a big winged snake which lives in lakes and causes storms. In the region of Knjaževac the ala is described as a giant **three headed** snake which can fly. In one mouth it carries nymphs and winds, in the other various diseases, and in the third evil deeds. In some other regions the Ala is a giant sea monster which creates big waves and eats people. Every Ala is considered to be a big gluttonous being, loud

and huge, which eats or drinks everything it comes across. They are said to live in caves, lakes, in great trees, mountains or among the stars. They are generally malevolent beings, but sometimes they appear as benevolent beings as well.

As creatures who nurture the land and the crops of people, until they are disturbed or killed, after which the land loses its fertility. The malevolent ones usually appear in the hot part of the year, bringing storms and hail, devastating the crops, stealing cattle or drinking their milk, even capturing people and drinking their blood.

For protection against an Ala the people took out a wooden chair in front of the house, and placed on it bread, salt, a knife and an axe turned with the head towards the sky. Or in some areas they threw stones towards the direction from where the wind blew. This is all imitative magic, as the stone and the axe are the weapon of Perun. During thunder and hail storms the Ala and the dragons fought in the sky, and when a dragon would defeat an ala she would hide in a tree. It is said that mice, bats, flies, snakes, lizards and rats are created from the body of a dead Ala. Like the Lamja, the Ala as well attempts to eat the Sun and the Moon, and besides her opponents being the dragon people, the most common is Saint Ilya. It was also believed that the Ala can interfere in people's destinies, take the shape of a human or an animal. The Ala can appear as an old woman who lives in a hut deep within the forest, and she can punish or reward people who encounter her, which links her very much to the Russian Baba Yaga.

So for example in one tale a girl, chased away by her evil step mother, wanders off to the house of Ala. She calls her "mother" and she does all the chores in her house, after which the Ala rewards her with a chest of gold. When her step-mother sees that, she sends her own daughter to the same hut, but because she is rude the Ala gave her a chest of poisonous snakes.

Here we can also connect the saying that the Ala keeps great amounts of treasure in her cave, just like the Lamja. This is a tale which in essence describes the process of reincarnation, and it can be found in many variations across all of Europe, with the place of the Ala being taken by an old woman, a fairy, a white woman, Baba Yaga, a dragon, or a bear.

The fact that the Ala appears in such a role indicates that she was, or rather is, an ancient Goddess or God of the dead and the underworld. For example, it has been shown many times by different authors that Baba Yaga is a fairy tale adaptation of the great Slavic earth Goddess *Mokoš*, or rather her manifestation as the mother of the dead, known as *Vela*.

**Aždaja** –From the Avestan word *aži*, meaning „snake", or „dragon" probably brought to the Balkans by the Turks. According to the beliefs it is a huge serpentine winged being with several heads, like a lion's head, with a wide jaw, sharp teeth, and four legs with big claws. Usually they are described as having **three, seven or nine heads**, and that they blow fire or have a fiery tongue. They have a terrifying scream, big shining eyes, they are furious, gluttonous and eat everything they come across. They live in caves, lakes, deep waters or swamps, where they rise from and eat people's cattle. They are even said to live in hell and devour the sinful. Among the Croats, the Aždaja is like a huge fat snake which lives in swamps and eats people. At mount Dinara the Aždaja is described as a long serpent which devours people and cattle, and leaves a trail behind it „as if a huge tree was pulled", which is very interesting because it reminds us of *črt*, the "one who leaves a mark". The only way to kill the Aždaja is to cut off her head, and from its body are born flies, snakes, lizards, mice and rats. The Aždaja is also said to keep treasure in the depths of her cave. Likewise, it is said that the Aždaja attacks the sun when it is born in the east, but St. Ilya shoots her with lightning and scares her off, so she runs to hide in the water.

According to one tale Miloš Obilić wanted to build a monastery in the region of Brančevo, but in a dream St. George told him that first he has to kill the Aždaja which lives under Golubački Grad. Obilić cut all her three heads off and built the Tuman monastery. I don't know about you, but this tale reminds me of the ancient Greek myth of Appolo who killed the dragon Python at Delphi, before establishing his temple.

From what we can see based on the folk accounts, it makes sense why these three names – Lamja, Ala and Aždaja, are synonyms. They represent the same being. A giant winged, fire blowing, reptilian being with several big heads, shining eyes, wide jaws, sharp teeth, either with or without legs, and sharp claws. Closely related to the Christian devil. Living underground, under water, in trees or caves. Extremely gluttonous, eating the crops, animals and humans, bringing diseases and drinking or restraining all the waters of the earth. Possessing the power to change its shape, appears as an old woman and closely related to the ancient Slavic Goddess of the dead.

In all Slavic languages, **except** the South Slavic languages, such a being is called a „dragon", with the Slavic word *zmej, zmey, zmaj*, or something similar, and such a being is **always** related to the earth. This is why the Proto-Slavic words *zmьjь* („dragon") and *zmьja* („snake; serpent") are derived from the word *zemľa* („earth"). Therefore the term *zmьjь* is just an epithet of the chthonic deity, and it translates as „earthen ; of the earth." In the South Slavic languages the word „dragon" i.e. *zmej, zmey* or *zmaj,* began to be used for heroes such as Marko, Saint Ilya (Perun), or the dragon people, whereas the creatures which originally represented dragons were now called by names loaned either from Greek or Persian, such as *Lamja, Ala and Aždaja*. This is why the Ala appears as an ancient earth Goddess of the dead.

Therefore from now on whenever you read "dragon" you should understand that I refer to the real, original appearance of the dragon (*zmьjь)*, and *not* to the dragon people, or the South Slavic fiery dragons.

As we have seen by now, among the South Slavs besides these special dragon people, the main enemy of the dragon i.e. Lamja, Ala and Aždaja, was St.Ilya, and as I previously mentioned he is the Christian successor of Perun. Ilya, like Perun, was said to ride through the clouds on his chariot of fire or gold, pulled by horses or fiery dragons during storms, striking the malevolent dragons which brought hail, or caused drought. Thus he was regarded as the one which released the water from the sky.

„Грмеж. Свети Илија грми сос кочијата. Змеот фрла огин по ламњата и ако се скрије ламњата во нешчо; у човек, у камен или у шчо да било, ќе фрли змеот на тоа место стрела - сос острила од камен – и ако го погоди ќе го трешчи."
(Матев, 132)

"Thunder. Saint Ilya thunders with the chariot. The dragon throws fire at the lamja and if she hides in something; in man, in stone or in anything else, to that place the dragon will throw (shoot) an arrow – with a head of stone – and if he hits it, it will set it ablaze."

As we can see from this except, Saint Ilya, or more precisely Perun, was considered to be a fire dragon, thus making Prince Marko and all other heroes his incarnations.
This is also confirmed by the folk tale "Jana's Tombstone" which I spoke of in my first book, where the fire dragon who battles against the calf headed water dragon, lives on a mountain peak called Perun. It is no surprise then that Perun is called Fire Tsar in some Russian sources, and his opponent is the Snake Tsar.

The context in which the following Russian dialogue appears is similar to the previous Macedonian source, only here it's not a battle of Saint Ilya and a Lamja, but of God and the Devil:

"Гэто споруваў Бог зь нячисьциком:
Я цябе, каецъ, забъю!
— А як ты мяне забъёш: я схуваюся!
— Куды?
— Под чалавека!
— Я чалавека забъю, грèху ямỳ отпущу, а - цябе забъю!
— А я пот коня!
—Я й коня забъю, чалавека на гэтым месьци награжду, а цябе забъю!
— А я пот корову схуваюся!
— Я й корову забъю: хозяину на гэто место награжду, а цябе забъю
— Ну, дык я, каецъ, схуваюся у воду пот корч, пот колоду!
—Ну, там твое место, там сабе будз!"

"Thus quarreled God with the Unclean one:
I shall, 'tis said, kill you!
— And how shall you kill me: I shall hide!
— Where?
— Beneath a man!
— I shall kill a man, relieve him of sins, and then kill you!
— And I [shall hide] beneath a horse!
— I shall kill a horse too, compensate the man at once, and then kill you!
— And I shall hide beneath a cow!
— I shall kill a cow too, compensate the owner at once, and then kill you
— Well then, I shall, 'tis said, hide in water beneath a trunk,

*beneath a log!*
*— Well, there is your place, there you be!"*
(translation by Katičić)

**His place is below, under the tree, in the water.**

Vuk Karađić in his „Српски рјечник"recorded that „Кад гром удара, онда кажу да свети Илија, по заповјести Божијој, гађа ђавола."

„When thunder strikes, it is said that Saint Ilya, by God's order, shoots the devil."

A Russian source also tells that the devils are many, but they are struck down by Perun: „Их жа, бач, кольки ё! А их жа й Пярун бъé !"

"Them (i.e. the devils), look, how many they are! Them Pyarun kills!"

Now we are obviously dealing with very late accounts here, where much of the actual meaning of the old myths has degraded to superstition because of Christianity. But such accounts can be found across all Slavic lands, and they reflect the essence of the European thunder Gods. It is difficult at this moment not to think about Zeus' battle against the Titans, or Thor's battle with the Jötnar, especially when we know that their name means "gluttonous; greedy; consuming" which is the *main* characteristic of the Ala, Aždaja and Lamja i.e. the original Slavic dragon.

Since our mythology in essence is about reincarnation, these malevolent spirits, these devils, Jötnar, Titans and dragons which our thunder Gods kill, originally were a metaphor for the ancestors which are going to be reincarnated. And the one participating in the reincarnation ritual was none other than Perun, Thor and Zeus.

Yes, when the Christians gained power in Europe they made sure that the ancestral cult of the native Europeans was completely cut down, so they turned the ancestors into devils and demons. They turned the bear, which was the most primordial ancestral animal across all of Europe, into a devil. Well, the most common avatars of the Slavic God **Veles**, the male appearance of the previously mentioned Goddess Vela and the mythical opponent of Perun, were the bear, wolf and dragon. It is therefore no surprise that Veles was also turned into the devil. Tkadleček, the Czech novel written in the early XV century, puts the following exclamation into the mouth of the angry hero: *"Ký jest **črt**, aneb ký **veles**, aneb ký **zmek** tě proti mně zbudil?"*

*"What **devil**, or what **veles**, or what **dragon** incited you against me ?"*

The word *črt* ("devil") is, like *zmьjь*, just another pre-Christian attribute of Veles, derivied from Proto – Slavic *čъrtъ* "one who digs; makes a notch; leaves a mark", also the root for the word *kъrtъ* "mole" who as we know literally digs holes underground. This explains why in the Belarussian folklore we find the following sayings:
„Пярун забив змея." – *"Pyarun killed the dragon."* But also: „Пярун забив чорта." - "Pyarun killed the devil (*čort*). Of course *čort/ črt* only became the devil after Christianity, just like the name of *Velns*, or *Velnias* the Baltic cognate of the Slavic God Veles today literally means "devil".

However, these two attributes do not have cognates in the Indo-European languages, meaning that they probably appeared later in the Proto-Slavic vocabulary, thus making the Proto-Slavic word *ǫžь* ( "snake" ) the oldest term used for snake, or dragon and therefore the mythical opponent of Perun, since it stems from a PIE root with many mythological and linguistic cognates.[1]

---

[1] Some of them are the Latin *anguis*, Old High German *unc*, Avestan *ažiš* (cf. South Slavic *Aždaja*), Sanskrit *ahi*, all derived from the PIE root $h_1óg^{wh}is$, meaning "snake".

What we have seen so far reflects, in essence, the primordial Slavic myth of the battle between Perun and Veles, which occurs every time Veles restrains the waters of the world and causes drought. We will see later on, that Prince (Kraljević) Marko appears in the same mythological context, which is why it was necessary for all this to be said and understood beforehand.

In the folklore of Polesia a dragon is said to have the body of a snake and the head of a bear, which unites these two avatars of Veles, and explains why the South Slavic Lamja, Ala and Aždaja are said to have a reptilian body and always a big head with wide jaws and sharp teeth.

Veles is the god of the underworld, the ancestral spirits, sorcery, music, cattle, forests, animals, wealth, trade, travel and mischief. Essentially he is an avatar of the ancestors, and his realm lies *"beyond the sea"* where the birds and bees fly to during the winter, but also the ancestral spirits after death. This is why in the sacred geography of the Slavs, Veles was **always** related to lowlands, valleys, caves, trees and the holes in them, or their roots, just like the dragons among Slavs, and the Lamja, Ala and Aždaja among South Slavs. He lived **below**, under the sacred **tree**, near or in the **water.**

Like all other Europeans, Slavs had sacred trees, especially trees with wells or water springs underneath them, as attested in many accounts.

These wells or water springs are an equivalent of the Norse well under Yggdrasil, where Odin sacrificed his eye in order to drink from its waters, and they are the dwelling place of the "unclean one", of the "devil", as the Christians would say, but in reality simply the dwelling place of Mimir among the Norse, or **Veles** among Slavs. God, Saint Ilya, or simply **Perun** lived above, in the sky, on the top of the sacred tree, or on mountain peaks, in a fortress or city often described as white. This is evident from toponyms across all Slavic lands, and also the fact that in the pantheon of Prince Vladimir of Kiev, Veles was not placed among the other Gods, but below, near the marketplace, as Veles also governs trade.

Veles also appears as **Triglav** or **Trojan**, meaning "three headed" or "thrice", which is evident from the Zbruch idol, a IXth century idol found in the river Zbruch, Ukraine, but also recorded in Western Slavic historical sources, Eastern Slavic tales and South Slavic legends. Among the South Slavs Trojan always wears **black**, and rides a black horse, just like the black horse which was kept in the temple of Triglav among Western Slavs, whereas the horse of Sventovit (Perun) was white, just like his previously mentioned White City. They are Chernobog (the black God) and Belobog (the white God). Trojan also lives in caves, hollow trees of abandoned forts called Trojan town, all symbols of the underworld, and with his three heads he is said to *devour* people, animals and fish.

Again we see a strong resemblance to the Slavic dragon, and South Slavic Lamja, Ala and Aždaja. It is therefore obvious that Trojan / Triglav and Veles are the same deity. Just as Vela appears as a feminine side of Veles, so Trigla appears in the sources of Western Slavs as the female equivalent of Triglav.

The thrice Goddess is ultimately Mokoš i.e. the three Fates, known among Slavs as Rozhanitsi, Narechnici, Sudjenice and so forth, which govern the fates of people. Perhaps this is why the Ala was believed to interfere in people's destinies.

A three headed or thrice being, be it a dragon, giant, God or Goddess is always the adversary of the hero in the myths, folks and tales, not just of the Slavs but all of Europe.

Its thrice nature represents the three pregnancies through which the ancestor is reborn in the child, but also the three *times* – past, present and future, which are perceived by the human mind. In other words, she/he/it *is* time. It's the time which passes until the ancestor is reincarnated in a new body. The time which is transcended by the realization that it (time) is an illusion, and that our true nature is divine, immortal, as Perun.

It's how one reincarnates, how one becomes a "fiery dragon", for it is the meaning of all dragon-slayer myths, and in fact the meaning of all European myths and tales.

Even though most of this does not seem to have much in common with Prince Marko so far, you will eventually understand that it was indeed essential to go through the examples in which the mythological battle between Perun and Veles survived among the Slavs, especially in the south. And although the primary focus so far is put on Perun, that does not have to mean that Prince Marko inherited only Perun's characteristics. He probably inherited aspects of other gods, like Jarilo who was the predecessor of St. George, and he most likely even inherited some ancient elements from the Thracian Horseman, known as Sabazios among the Bryges and Thracians, whose name is derived from the Thracian word sabazias, meaning free. The word sabazias is a cognate of the Slavic word svoboda, meaning freedom, derived from the Proto- Slavic term *svobъ ("self; self – dependent", the root for the word *sebě – "oneself"), and from the Proto Indo-European root *swo- ("his own; self").

The –zios element in his name is derived from the PIE word *dyew ("sky; heaven; bright"). The three finger salute related to Sabazios is still used today among Serbs, and it was used as a sign of liberty during their revolts against the Ottoman empire.

Interestingly, the Thracian horseman was also called Perkos/Perkon (Περκος/Περκων), represented as a horseman hero facing a tree surrounded by a snake, or a goddess. And we shall see later on Marko will appear in the same scenario, beneath a tree facing a serpent, dragon or a fairy sometimes bearing the name of the ancient goddess Vela. Likewise the one example found in Varna, Bulgaria, he is given the epithet ΠΕΡΚΟΥΣ and ΠΕΡΚΩΝΙΣ i.e. Perkoys and Perkonis, all of which are etymologically identical to Perun, his Baltic equivalent Perkunas, and his Illyrian equivalent Perendi. This should be no surprise, since even the most reliable Roman (Byzantine) historians, like Theophylact Simocatta, clearly identify the Slvas as the Getae, stating that "this is the older name for the barbarians."

Therefore it is obvious that, as previously said, the European myths, Gods and heroes carry the same essence, the same epithets even, but expressed in a different way. And we also must bear in mind the fact that South Slavs are mostly and mainly descendants of the Paleo – Balkanic tribes, such as Thracians and Illyrians, so there could have been adaptations to the previous local cults. This is why later on the legends and songs of Kraljević Marko will be examined and explained independently, and compared to the myths of other deities only when it is required.

# The Mysteries

Assuming that you have read some of my two previous books "Chernobog's Riddles" and "The Sorcerous Spring", or at least the brilliant book by Marie Cachet entitled "The Secret Of The She – Bear" which gave me the key to unlock all these mysteries for you, I will not go in great detail to explain all the symbols which appear in our myths and fairy tales, and represent different stages of the reincarnation process. Because this is not the purpose of this book, I will just quickly tell you what you need to know before we continue to the tales and songs of Prince Marko.

Before the arrival of the Abrahamic worldview in Europe, we native Europeans had a worldview which was cyclical and centered around reincarnation, which we expressed in our myths, tales and rituals. Unlike the modern Europeans poisoned by consumerist propaganda, the ancient Europeans valued quality over quantity, and this was embodied in their understanding of reincarnation. Not everyone could reincarnate, but they made sure that only the kind, brave, honourable and wise would return to life, whereas the weak, cowardly and deceitful would fade away into oblivion. This is why the honourable were given a proper burial, ensuring their passage to the realm of the dead through various ceremonies, whereas the dishonourable were not given a proper burial, but instead were thrown into places which were considered "between the two worlds", so to speak, so that they could not reincarnate. For example, the Germanic people threw their scum into bogs, as recorded by Tacitus. By doing so they preserved what was valuable and good, thus a kin, a tribe would be composed of good quality people whose traits would live on forever.

The process of reincarnation was not only physical, to be re-born through the biological womb of the mother, but also spiritual. The reincarnation process is divided in three cycles which we will simply refer to as "three pregnancies" through which the child needs to pass in order to be reborn. The first pregnancy is the biological one, which ends when the baby is born. The second pregnancy lasts until the child reaches the age of 7, the age of reason, when the child is weaned and his permanent teeth start to grow, meaning that it can eat real food. Until then it is under the protection of the mother, and therefore it is considered to be symbolically in her womb. The third pregnancy is the final reincarnation ritual.

This means that when a child would be old enough, and that was usually between 7 and 8 years old, it would participate in a reincarnation ritual through which it would acquire its real name i.e. the name of the honourable dead – of himself in previous lives. Among the Slavs this remained a ritual in which the child at the age of seven would descend into a cave taking with it only a candle. In the cave a sorcerer impersonating the god Veles would welcome the child and kindle its candle, after which the child went outside and placed the candle on the ground along with the candles of other children, forming a fiery ring. Later the children would step into the ring and have their first haircut, even if it was just a small piece of hair, and receive their real names, names which belonged to the honourable dead – themselves in previous lives. Among some Slavs only the hair cutting part of the ritual was preserved, but the children always received their real names at the age of seven, and before that they had a substitute name, so to speak. The cutting of the hair is a symbolic act of rebirth, it mimics the cutting of the umbilical cord, for the hair is related to Veles/Triglav, who is represented as having very long hair and beard. This is why Slavic sorcerers, known as *volhvs* (akin to druids) were obliged to let their hair and beard grow very long.

The name *volhv*, derived from Old Church Slavonic вълхвъ is a cognate of the Norse *völva*, is related to the word влъшьба, meaning "sorcery", and is ultimately derived from the same root as the name of Veles / Volos.

The volhvs were the midwives of the mind, that is to say they were the ones responsible for giving birth to the ancestor within the child, which is why they led the reincarnation rituals, told the tales, sang the songs and helped the children understand the meaning behind them, thus helping them find back to themselves. Like all European sorcerers, the volhvs wore long white dresses, which is a female clothing, but they wore since they were the spiritual midwives. They also had a staff which was essentially a bough from the sacred tree. In a way they were the predecessors of the post-Christian godfathers and godmothers who give a name to the child, although in fairy tales and myths their role can be taken by fairies, like the fairy godmother of Cinderella, or bees.

Their role of singing songs and telling tales brings them close to the role of bards, which is why in the Polish language sorcery is called *gusła* and it is the root for the word *guślarz*, meaning sorcerer, synonymous to volhv. But in the South Slavic languages a *guslar* is a village bard who plays an instrument called *gusla*, a single-stringed lute like instrument with a bowl like body, held vertically in the lap and played with a bow, originating among the South Slavs. The Serbo-Croatian *gusla* (the instrument) and the Polish *gusła* (sorcery) are derived from Proto-Slavic *gǫsti* – to sing; to howl; to cry, from Proto-Balto-Slavic *gaustei*, from Proto-Indo-European *gewH-* ("to call, invoke, cry"). Therefore the sorcerer would sit under the sacred tree and he would sing the hymns of the Gods, the myths which were supposed to be understood.

However, the Old Slavic or Old Russian *gusli* was used to refer to any stringed instrument, which explains why what the Russians call *gusli* and what the Serbs and Croats call *gusla* refers to completely different type of instruments which were used to sing the myths, or rather to invoke the Gods. This is also why in the Rus' epic entitled *The Lay of Igor's Campaign* the bard Boyan is called "grandson of *Volos*", and interestingly his name is derived from the Proto-Slavic word *bajati* ("to tell") which is also the root for the Proto-Slavic *бајъка* ("myth; fable"). Therefore the name Boyan means "story teller; bard", and he by default is a sorcerer, because he plays the *gusla*, hence the nickname *"grandson of Volos"*.

Now, the claim that the songs of Prince Marko were indeed mythological and not historical, makes more sense when we know that they were sang by a **guslar**, playing a **gusla**. In other words, they are remnants of the ancient myths sang by the old volhvs – sorcerer bards, as tools to **reincarnate the minds** of the ancestors in the children who understood their meaning.

In the Stone Age the reincarnation ritual was done by the descent of the child into the cave where the dead was buried, where the child used an antler of a deer to dig out the grave and collect the skull, thigh bone and the items the dead was buried with. Of course those items were his, from a previous life, and as explained before, in the Stone Age the Neanderthals put a biface (the weapon of the thunderer) on the chest of the dead with which the child would kindle a fire, symbolically re-kindling his own heart. The oldest evidence of such a ritual can be found in France in the Neanderthal burial at Le Regourdou, which is more than 70,000 years old, where the upper part of the skull is missing, and the thigh bone of the buried man was replaced by that of a cave bear. This is because the oldest pre – historic cult in Europe is that of the cave bear, which later evolved, changed and adapted, but its essence remained the same, and its traces can be found among various European Gods, rituals, songs and tales.

The bear was the oldest venerated animal in Europe, for it was considered a tutelary ancestor of the Neanderthals which inhabited Europe. Their whole understanding of the universe was centered around this animal, for the womb of the great She-Bear was not just the cave, as the womb of the earth, but also the universe as a whole. The bear was the bearer of the universe, its upholder, its axis.

This understanding remained among the Europeans much after the Gods acquired an anthropomorthic appearance, only then it was associated with a certain God, like Veles / Triglav among the Slavs, whose appearance has been confirmed many times to be a bear. This is why in the Serbian folklore it is said that the spirits of the dead travel across the Milky Way in order to reach the otherworld. This is the "great sea" which needs to be crossed in order to arrive to the ancestral resting place, the realm of Veles, which explains why Serbs called the Milky Way *Jovanova struga*, meaning "St. John's current/stream". This sea, this stream, this watery abyss in the sky is the same amniotic waters of the womb from where the child arrives, whilst the caves and later burial mounds were made to represent this womb. We find the same pattern in the sacred geography of Slavs, where the toponyms associated with Veles, or the graveyard of villages are always across a river.

So you see the cycle – the child is born, it is an ancestor arriving from beyond the great sea, or river, and when the grown man dies he travels across the great sea again, to eventually be reborn.

Having a mostly agrarian culture, the other name for the Milky Way which the Serbs and other South Slavs used is *Kumova Slama*, meaning "Godfather's Hay". This is related to the name "St. John's Stream" because in the Serbian folklore St.John is a patron of godfathers, obviously since he baptised Jesus, but as such he inherited many of Veles' attributes. Another thing which links this to Veles is that in the Slavic folklore we often find a connection between threshing floors and the sky, whilst the central pillar of the threshing floor was associated with the star Polaris, the axis of the sky. Well, each year after the harvest Slavs use the last stalk of wheat to knit a "beard" which they call "grandfather's beard", "God's beard", or in Russia "Beard of Veles", which they put on the central pillar of the threshing floor, representing Veles-Triglav himself. He is the bear, axis of the cosmos, its bearer and upholder, as shown on the

Zbruch idol. Hence why in Slavic folk songs sang during the harvest, a bear is mentioned to sit upon a hay stack and admire its beard, which of course is not a bearded bear, but Veles himself. This explains why in South Slavic embroidery the rhomboid symbol usually placed upon a woman's womb is called "threshing floor". It also explains why in Slavic fairy tales and toponyms we often find threshing floors made of copper, silver, gold or crystal, also threshing floors called "God's threshing floor", "Threshing floor of fairies", where dragons, fairies, or even Baba Yaga lives, and where the heroes of the tales go be reincarnated.

So what is reincarnation? And should you remember all the details of your previous lives? Do you remember all the details of your life from one day ago? Or maybe from one week ago? No, you do not, because you don't need to. But if you experienced something which changed your life forever, by awakening some good qualities within you, your courage, love and will, or made you wiser, even if you don't remember this moment, you will still possess the uplifting qualities. You will become them, and you will be able to nourish them, to grow better. Therefore, you don't need to remember everything from your previous lives either. So what part of you actually reincarnates? Let's start with what doesn't first.

Everything temporary and prone to change through time which is related to "You" i.e. the Ego, will disappear eventually. That includes your memories which naturally fade away, and your idea of yourself built in life. If you are honourable, you will be remembered by your deeds, your name will be remembered and eventually you will be reborn. This is how the name of the historical Marko Mrnjavčević ended up being used in a totally mythological context. There is a part of you, or of the psyche if you will, which does reincarnate, simply because it always is. It was never born, nor does it die. It is neither a subject to time, nor space. It is the sum of you i.e. your ancestors and descendants, and it is simply the source of all life.

In the myths this source of immortality to which you (the hero/deity) come back to over and over again, is represented by the tree of life (the most common avatar of the placenta), the golden apples which grow on it, the spring below it, a God or Goddess, an animal or mythical creature, and so forth.

The myths are about you. They are riddles whose aim is to help you realize who you really are i.e. to help you overcome the fear of change and death, by understanding your true nature, which is free and immortal. Despite the sum being pure white light, in the myths represented as the Sky father, biologically it is the placenta. Yes, because just as you are able to drink from the source and realize your immortality, like Prince Marko drank from the "immortal water", so the baby "drinks" the blood from the placenta. The placenta is composed of the father's DNA and represents the biological appearance of the tree of life, which is as we said the sum of you, centered in the ever present axis mundi, right here and now, in the present moment. In eternity.

Perun sits above the tree on his throne, he is the foetus. Veles is the dragon, the ancestor, the umbilical cord, in the roots of the tree near the water, the sacred spring – the blood. He restrains the waters, while Perun releases them and drinks from them - foetus nourished by the blood. He kills Veles, the umbilical cord is cut, Perun is reborn. Veles is Triglav, the thrice one, restraining the eternal psyche in the illusionary realm of time - past, present and future. Perun kills Veles and transcends time, reborn in the present moment, enlightened to eternity. This is what the myths are about.

***Blood = Fire = Gold = Light = Honour = Spirit = Memory = Enlightenment.***

Since the source is the sum, then it must be composed of something. But what's it composed of? From you and your family, tribe and race, as one kin, one blood, one honour and spirit. Individually, as your physical appearance is composed from all the various parts of your ancestors, so is your spirit. Talents, weaknesses, advantages, and so forth. Everything your ancestors were and everything they did, from instincts to trauma, is reflected in you, consciously or not. Some characteristics and abilities survive because they were cultivated, others disappear or sink in the unconscious, until they are revived by an external trigger, such as a certain environment, lifestyle, myth, and so on.

They are the memories, so to speak. Even genes go recessive and reappear after some time. This fact alone is enough for one to understand that who you *think* you are, is not who you *really* are. This is why our ancestors had traditions, that is to say a way to help their offspring reach the source of immortality through myths, tales, songs and rituals, and pass on what was valuable, good, useful (skills), and honourable. This is what we call memories - the uplifting qualities through which your experience of previous lives is expressed, your accumulated honour which literally gives you good luck. Among the Slavs this individual and family luck, fate, honour or slava ("glory") was embodied in the concept called Rod among Eastern Slavs, and Usud among South Slavs.

In my book "Chernobog's Riddles" i examined the possibility of Rod being an ancient equivalent of the Sky God, and even tried to equate him to Perun, although i made it clear that such a claim is impossible to prove. And, i was right. I based my claim on the following XV century Christian source, which is the only source implying that Rod was possibly a deity"... *So not Rod sitting in the air, throwing clods to the Earth, from which children are born... The creator of all is God, not Rod*".

However, to say that Rod was a God, let alone the Sky Father is wrong, because we have no way to prove it. Offerings to Rod & Rozhanitsas (=Fates; Norns; midwives) were given when a child was born, because they determined the child's fate (luck) on the third night after the birth. The midwives who helped the child to be born could literally "read" the placenta and determine if the child would be healthy or not.

Rod's name means "kin", and that is exactly what he is = the sum of the kin, presiding over the luck of one's life. The Rozhanitsas have the same role, but they are also the midwives, biological and spiritual. Rod is only mentioned among Eastern Slavs, whereas among the Southern Slavs he is known as Usud, and the "Fates" are called Suđenice (sometimes also Narečnici), both of which mean "fate; destiny", because that is what they represent. This is also evident by the fact that sometimes in the Slavic languages the Greek term "τύχη" (týchi, "luck") is translated as "rod", and "εἱμαρμένη" (eímarméni, "destiny") is translated as a "rozhanitsa". Therefore Rod/Usud (kin / destiny) is the ancestral sum which is composed of the collective honour and glory, and as such he determines the luck and destiny of the individual, or the family. This luck is in the songs and tales represented as a follower, either as a fairy, a beautiful maiden (good luck), or an ugly one (bad luck). In one tale in which a man goes to find Usud and ask him why he is so unfortunate, Usud is represented as living far away beyond a river, and he determines the fortune of men by the amount of fortune he has in the day. His riches move in a cycle, from filthy rich to filthy poor, so depending on the day one is born, so shall be his fate. Fortune, or rather gold, is a symbol of honour and glory, ancestral memory, and all the positive qualities which go along with it, as previously explained.

Therefore, Perun remains the Slavic Sky God, whereas the essence of the Slavic ancestral cult was represented through Rod/Usud, who was not venerated as a God, but simply as the sum of the collective honour, and the protector of the kin.

# I
## THE BIRTH OF KRALJEVIĆ MARKO

Hunting was Vukašin the king,
Hunting he was, three white days.
When the fourth morning dawned,
Sat the king on a cold stone,
Near the stone his spear stuck in earth,
To the spear his horse he tied,
Thus he spoke to his horse:
„Oh, unfortunate king Vukašin!
I could not even see a bird,
Let alone hunt something today,
I'm hungry, thirsty and hungry!"
Yet to the king a vila spoke:
„You are wise, king Vukašin,
You are wise, but speak foolishly,
Below you is a green lake,
At the lake sits the vila Mandalina,
She will tell you how to hunt,
However, she takes a heavy price:
The arms and muscles of heroes!"
When Vukašin the king heard that,
He mounted his fine steed,

And rode through the green hill[2],
Good luck was on his side.
On the green hill, at the lake,
At the lake sat vila Mandalina,
But a dream had taken the vila.
Came close Vukašin the king,
He stole her shirt and crown,
Thus rode towards his white palace.
When the vila woke up from her dream,
She was sad and deeply troubled,
For her shirt and crown were missing.
She flew across the green hill,
And she met Vukašin the king,
So she spoke to him softly:
„Give me, king, the shirt and crown,
I shall do you many favors!"
Answered her king Vukašin:
I do not want, oh vila, any gift,
But you shall be my beloved!"
She was sad and deeply troubled,
She went with him to the white palace,
Married her, Vukašin the king.
Two sons she bore him:
The first was Kraljević Marko
And the second, Andrija the weak.

---

[2] The original word in the song whch i translate as „hill" is *gora*, and in the south Slavic languages it is used for any elevated and forested place, so it can be translated as „hill", „mountain" and „forest".

# Meaning

As you can see this is a purely mythological song describing the birth of Kraljević Marko by a vila. A vila is a fairy which is present in the folklore of South Slavs, Slovaks and Czechs, whereas among other Slavs we find similar beings with different names and characteristics, such as the Russian Rusalka for example. The vila is imagined as a beautiful blonde girl in a long white dress, usually with wings, a bow and arrows. In the folklore they can appear as malevolent and benevolent, sometimes even as blood sisters, followers and helpers of the heroes, like the vila who advised king Vukašin where to go. In fact every hero is said to have a vila as a blood sister, including Marko as we will see later on, but girls from the folklore can also have a vila as their blood sister. In essence vilas are ancestral spirits, akin to the Norse elves, and according to folk accounts they could take possession of people and do various things through them, most often healing, or they could appear in people's dreams and instruct them how to become the village healer.

At first glance this song speaks of Marko's birth, but in essence it describes the process of reincarnation. Marko is the reincarnated ancestor. He is both Vukašin and the vila, naturally since they are his parents, but also because Vukašin is the participant in the reincarnation ritual, and Marko is simply Vukašin reborn. The vila is the ancestor, or the ancestral spirit if you will, which is sleeping *below* near the *lake*. In other words she is the dead ancestor residing in the burial mound, hence why she wants to kill the heroes who ask for advice.

Vukašin is the hungry and thirsty hunter, the child which seeks to be reborn. He hunts for three days, representing the three symbolic pregnancies, but also the time which he transcends. On the dawn of the fourth day he is taken to the grave by a vila i.e. he is called by the ancestor – himself.

In the grave he finds the dead ancestor, the sleeping vila – his other half, and collects the burial items – the crown (luminosity; memory; enlightenment) and the shirt (the body). The crown is also a replacement of the pre-historic deer antlers used to dig up the grave. They are essential items for the vila to have her power, which of course means that they are essential items for Vukašin to be reborn, for they are his life force. In the end Vukašin, the child, marries the Vila – he is reunited with the ancestral spirit, with himself. And from this marriage of the two opposites Marko is reborn.

## II
## KING MARKO AND VOLKAŠIN

This adventure of Marko has been recorded as a song and as a tale, with slight differences but nevertheless important for a better understanding of the symbols. For this reason i will present you with the tale and include some verses of the song which are important.

**The tale begins:**

Evrosima, the mother of Marko was pregnant and she gave birth to a male child, which made king Volkašin very happy. He took the child to church to get baptised immediately, before even tasting its mother's milk, and they gave him the name Marko. On the third night of Marko's birth Volkašin invited many guests to celebrate the birth of the boy. They drank and ate, and everyone fell asleep except Volkašin. On the stroke of midnight the three Fates called Narečnici came, to bestow the child's fate. One of them asked "What kind of fate shall we give him?" The second replied "We should bestow him with great luck, for he is the king's son." The third said "Marko will be a hero above all heroes, and when he grows up he will break the bones of his father". Upon hearing this Volkašin felt very bad, so he took Marko, he placed him in a basket and he threw him in the river Vardar to drown, so he would save himself from the words of the Fates.

There was a shepherd near the river which noticed the basket, and the child crying in it. Carefully he went into the river and he took the basket, so he brought the child to his wife. They kept him well for seven, eight, ten years, but they did not know that his fate was to become a hero. When Marko went out to play with other children he would always beat them up, for which the other villages complained: „Where did you find this little devil which beats up our kids? Find a solution for him!" So the shepherd, who also had cows, sent Marko to take care of the village calves. He was their herdsman for some years, but then they started running away, so he took the stick and beat them up. When his step-father understood what he did, he was furious and so he chased him away from his home forever. Marko then went to live in the sand and near the river Vardar.

One day a man was having a wedding[3], he had matchmakers, his witness would be King Volkašin, but he did not have a best man to accompany the bride. It was difficult to find a best man in those times, because all kinds of bandits came from the mountains. All the matchmakers would run away, but the best man had an oath to protect the bride, dead or alive. Because they could not find a best man, the godmother said "Go and whoever you find first take him as a best man." So they went and found Marko sitting along the river, and took him as a best man. They sat him next to the bride and whilst passing through a forest, a Black Arab crossed their way. All the matchmakers ran away, only Marko and the bride remained, so the Arab told him: "Give me the bride and the gifts, or you will die young!" Marko replied "I have no wedding gifts, I only protect the bride. If you want, let's fight! I will leave my head here, but I won't leave the bride!" Thus Marko fought and killed the black Arab, by cutting off his head.

In the song this is described in the following way:

> When they were returning,
> And passed through the forest green,
> A beast appeared,
> A beast, by God, with three heads,
> Which frightened all the matchmakers,
> And took away their gifts.
> From behind the two best men,

---

[2] In the song this is Relja Šestokrila (Hrelja Ohmućević).

> They lead the lovely bride,
> The beast asked for the bride,
> To the best men she said:
> - Leave, best men,
> Leave me the young bride,
> And you will go alive.

The matchmakers, the witnesses and the other best men ran away, leaving only Marko to battle the beast:

> The beast fought with Marko,
> Three hours they fought,
> Until Marko toppled the beast,
> He cut his three beastly heads,
> Which stole all the gifts.

***Continuing:***

When Marko decapitated the Black Arab, he took his head and went where the other guests were, as well as where the wedding celebration was supposed to be. There he found everyone eating, drinking and weeping for the death of Marko and the bride. He took the head and stood up on the table where they ate, so the guests got frightened and wanted to run away, but he said: „Shut up and eat, or i will cut all your heads as well!" They continued eating, and then Marko took the Arab's head, placed it in front of the godfather and said: „What kind of a godfather are you, leaving the bride and running away ?" The godfather was his father, king Volkašin, but Marko was unaware of that, so he hit him with his mace and broke all his bones. Volkašin then asked him „Which family do you come from, child ? Who are your mother and father ?" to which Marko replied „I have no father, the river Vardar is my mother." The king then remembered what the Fates said many years ago, so he explain to Marko that he is his real father. Marko was sorry to break his bones, he apologized, they kissed and lived happily.

## Meaning

This tale can be compared to many European fairy tales, but also many myths of the ancient world, as the mytheme of the child abandoned by his parents, in a river or any other place, which in the end grows to be a hero and kills his own father, because that is its destiny, is a very popular one. Yes, when Marko breaks the bones of his father he actually kills him, but we are obviously dealing with a later adaptation of the original myth.

Marko and his father are the same individual split in two, which is why in the end they will be reunited. In this tale Marko is the ancestor who is going to be reborn, which ulitimately happens through the death of his father. This was the meaning of the prophecy of the Narečnici - Fates.

Marko is thrown in the water to drown, but end up being saved by a shepherd. All children arrive from the water, or as we said before, from beyond the great sea. Therefore, Marko's appearance in the basket while floating in the water is a metaphor of the baby which is inside of the womb, and floats in the amniotic fluid. The first pregnancy ends when the shepherd rescues him, which also marks the beginning of the second pregnancy. In the myths the shepherd always takes the role of the ancestor, and we see the same thing here where the shepherd becomes Marko's stepfather. Despite the confusing amount of years which are mentioned in the tales, at this stage Marko is the child just before the age of seven, and you will see later that I am right. This is also represented by the fact that Marko becomes a herdsman of calves, which are of course suckled by cows. The cow is always a symbol of the mother, because the gestation period of both cows and European women is nine months. Therefore, this moment in the tale represents Marko as a child just before it is weaned. He is the calf being suckled, until he beats up the calves. This means that he is no longer dependant on his mother, but is the child at the age of 7 ready to participate in the reincarnation ritual. In the tale this is described as him being an orphan, living in the mud and dirt near the river. Like Cinderella who before transforming into a princess is dirty and covered in ashes, so Marko is dirty and covered in mud before appearing at the wedding party as the handsome young protector of the bride. He, like Cinderella, is the 7 year old child, masked and covered in ash to symbolically imitate the dead, before entering the underworld in order to reincarnate himself in his full splendour.

Marko is the child in the stage of the third pregnancy. Here we have the classic mytheme of the dragon attempting to steal the princess and the hero who rescues her. It is noteworthy that in one version Marko's opponent appears as a black Arab, whilst in the other as a three headed beast. The black Arab is just a symbolic adaptation to the time in which the tale was told, because the biggest threat to people back then really were Arabs and Turks from the Ottoman Empire. The Arab is not described as black just because Arabs really are darker than Europeans, but especially because he has a chthonic character which links him directly to Chernobog – the black god. That's why in the other version Marko battles a three headed beast, which is without a doubt a dragon, akin to the previously mentioned Ala, Lamja and Aždaja, who essentially represent the black three headed God Veles – the ancestor. To strengthen my claim I will simply present you with the verses of the song „The Wedding Of Mircheta The Warlord" where the Arab crossing their path is described as:

> „The Arab had three black heads,
> From the first blew a cold wind,
> From the second a fire burned,
> And his third head spoke..."

And the proof that the Arab really did replace the dragon lies in the verses of the song „Marko Kraljević and the dragon" where Marko tells his mother when he was most frightened. It was during the wedding of Janko of Sibiu, when along the way to the bride's new home a dragon crossed their path:

> „When we were at the mountain of Skolove,
> Where mothers mourn their sons,
> Appeared a three headed dragon,
> Three headed, six winged."

The bride is the spirit of the ancestor, and the gifts which the Arab-beast steals are the objects within the grave which the child would recollect. So, Marko decapitates the beast – the umbilical cord is cut; the child collects the ancestral skull from the grave. He rescues the princess – he is reunited with the ancestral spirit. He returns the stolen gifts – the ancestral memories; blood of the placenta; the objects of the grave. And in the end he kills his father, which is just another way to say that he becomes him. That's why they recognize each other in the end. Marko is reborn.

*King Marko, the dragon slayer*

## III
## PRINCE MARKO & THE FAIRY'S MILK

This tale and the verses of another version which we will compare, tell us how Prince Marko acquired his strength. It will also confirm that when Marko was a cowherd he indeed was at the age of 7, as I previously claimed, since this tale is directly linked to the previous, and in my opinion an inseparable element of it. Let's begin with the verses first:

> Grew Marko, grew and grew up,
> Grew and became the age of **seven**,
> Thus he went to be a cowherd.
> He took them to graze at the lake,
> There he heard the scream of a child.

Here it is then, Marko at the age of seven becoming a cowherd. Totally normal for such young children, isn't it? Of course not! It's a metaphor for the seven year old child participating in the reincarnation rite. The song goes on to say that Marko found a crying baby whom he gave water and kept in the shade until its mother, a Vila, returned and as a token of gratitude suckled Marko with her milk, thus giving him superhuman strength. The following tale however contains more archaic symbols which go in favour of my claim.

**The tale begins:**
Marko went after the calves, but on the way he noticed a big tree and a huge, furious snake crawling upon it. So Prince Marko hit it with his stick, and killed the snake. On that tree the fairies had a nest where their little fairy babies were, but the

snake always ate them. When Marko killed the snake the vila immediately came, and when she saw that Marko saved her children she asked him "Marko, what do you want in return for saving my children from this snake? So Marko said "Nothing. All the kids are beating me up. I want to be a hero so I can beat them up too." To which the fairy replied "Come here!" She removed her shirt, and breastfed him with her milk. Then she told him "Go shake that tree, let's see if you can remove it!" Marko went to the tree, he shook it, left, right, nothing. He couldn't remove it. "Come here and have some more of my milk" said the vila to Marko, and afterwards when he tried to remove the tree, he lift it up with its roots and threw it on the other side. "Now you have enough strength!" said the vila to Marko.

He then went to the other cowherd children and when one of them wanted to beat him up, Marko grabbed his hand and threw him two hundred meters away.

## Meaning

It's obvious to us now that Marko gained his strength by doing a good deed while he was a cowherd at his stepfather, at the age of seven. This also explains why later on Marko was able to defeat the three headed black Arab-beast. The vila who gives her milk to Marko exactly represents the breastfeeding mother nurturing her child until it is ready to participate in the reincarnation ritual. She is the sum of the ancestors, whilst Marko's superhuman strength represents the power of the accumulated honour successfully transferred into the new body of the ancestor.

The tree of course stands for the placenta, the baby fairies are another symbol of the foetus, whilst the blood thirsty snake is the umbilical cord which is cut upon birth.

# IV
## Wedding songs, customs and myths

The wedding songs from the cycle of Marko's epics follow a similar pattern, some of which contain more symbolic verses than others, but generally they all follow the same structure.

Some person, usually a genuine historical person, is asking for the hand of a girl which lives in a distant land. They gift each other, usually an apple is exchanged between them, as that is the ancient European custom which we find in many myths. After some time the bride needs to be taken from her father's home to the home of her new husband. Accompanied by various historical people which have a certain role in the wedding, Marko is always the best man whose duty is to protect the bride. Along the way from her old home they are met by an adversary who takes the wedding gifts and wants to take the princess as well, but he is defeated by the hero and the bride is escorted safely to her new home.

Interestingly, in the past this was not just a mythological motif, but reality during the weddings. In Serbia, Montenegro and Bosnia there are many places which are called *svatovsko groblje* „the graves of the matchmakers"[4] usually located in isolated places with old stone tombstones, quite often just big stones, where according to folk accounts lie the dead matchmakers of weddings which happened many years ago. Because people lived in closed communities made up of family members, the men who were supposed to get married usually had to search for a wife in another village, community or tribe. For this they organized a large procession of „matchmakers" with a leader called *vojvoda* „war leader", thus literally making them an army whose role

---

[4] In the South Slavic languages a wedding is called *svatba* or *svadba,* derived from the word *svat* "matchmaker", but also a title for the parents whose children are getting engaged, derived from Proto-Slavic *\*svatъ* "kin".

was to go to the bride's home and escort her back to her new home. They had a flag bearer and they were armed to the teeth because many dangers could be encountered along the way, but also because in most cases they had to take away the bride by force.

This is still a tradition among some South Slavs during the wedding ceremonies, where the groom and his band of matchmakers are being fought by the bride's brothers, cousins and other relatives. Most often this is done symbolically these days, but sometimes it can get rough as well. As an example, on the wedding day of my parents, when my father went with his men to fetch my mother, the „battle" stopped after they broke and smashed the door to the ground.

In the tale „King Marko and Volkašin" we already examined some of the symbols and explained how the song essentially speaks of reincarnation. We also saw that what once was a three headed dragon eventually became a three headed black Arab, but here I want to present you with some more evidence. The following song „Marko ends the wedding tax" does not have a similar pattern to „King Marko and Volkašin", but it is important that we understand this song first before we move on to other more similar songs.

In the song Marko arrives at the plain of Kosovo and notices a beautiful maiden whose hair is becoming white, so he asks what's her misfortune. She replies:

> „Dear brother, unknown hero,
> I have lost my fortune,
> Neither because of me, nor my mother,
> Nor because of my old father,
> Yet I have lost my fortune:
> It's been nine years

> As the Arab *came from overseas*,
> He took Kosovo from the tsar,
> And performed an evil:
> Kosovo provides him with food and drink.
> Another evil he performed:
> Woman who marries, thirty ducats,
> Man who marries, thirty four ducats."

The black Arab restricts the wedding ceremonies by demanding a high tax. But that's not the only thing he demans:

> I would not despair for it,
> That we are unable to marry young,
> And marry young heroes,
> But here is a greater trouble,
> A greater evil he demands:
> At night goes a young maiden,
> And the maiden, the Arab loves,
> But a bride the Arab's servants.
> The whole Kosovo was aligned,
> And gave him young girls,
> Now my unfortunate turn has come,
> To go to the Arab tonight,
> To be his beloved tonight,
> So I think and I wonder,
> Dear God, what shall i do?
> Either I unlucky shall jump in the water,
> Or shall I hang myself young?

> I'd rather lose my head,
> Than make love to the enemy!"

The dragon who restricts the waters and demands a maiden sacrifice each day is a very common mytheme in the South Slavic folklore, and I have shown many such examples in my previous book „The Sorcerous Spring". We have already seen that the Lamja, Ala and Aždaja have exactly this role. In essence it is a remnant of the ancient Slavic myth where Veles in the form of a three headed dragon restricts the waters of the world, and Perun releases them as he defeats Veles. However, here we have an adaptation of the myth to the time and the circumstances of the people, so instead of a dragon restricting the waters we find an Arab restricting weddings, and instead of demanding a maiden to eat he demands a maiden to rape. When Marko asks where he can find the Arab's courtyard, the maiden of Kosovo replies:

> „It is not a courtyard, but a tent.
> Look down, through the Kosovo field,
> Where that silk flag hangs,
> That's the tent of the black Arab,
> Around him is a green field,
> The whole of it is adorned with heads,
> There has not been a week yet,
> Since the damn Arab decapitated,
> Seventy seven heroes,
> Unfortunate grooms of Kosovo.
> The Arab has fourty servants,
> Who keep guard around him."

The Arab lives *down*, therefore same as the dragon, same as Veles, in the realm of the dead, represented here as the seventy seven dead grooms. When Marko went in his tent, the Arab is described as:

> The Arab sits, drinks cool wine,
> Served by a young maiden.
> God's help Marko invoked:
> „May God help, dear lord!"
> The Arab replied politely:
> „Healthy, hero, unknown hero!
> Come, let's drink wine,
> And tell me why you came."
> Thus spoke Marko Kraljević:
> „I have no reason to drink with you,
> But I come to you for a good reason,
> Very good, cannot be better:
> I asked a maiden's hand,
> My matchmakers are left on the road,
> I came, I brought tax money,
> To give you money, to take the girl,
> And that nobody stands in my way,
> So tell me, what's the price?"
> The Arab answered nicely:
> „You know it already,
> A woman who marries, thirty ducats,
> A man who marries, thirty four,
> You seem like a dueling champion,
> It won't be bad if you pay a hundred!"
> Marko searched in his pockets,

And threw three ducats before the Arab:
„Trust me, I have nothing more,
But if you would wait for me,
To return with the bride,
There I shall be gifted,
I shall give you all the gifts,
The gifts for you, the bride for me."
Screamed the Arab like a furious snake:
„There's no credit here!
You don't pay, and you mock me!"
He took his heavy mace,
And hit Kraljević Marko,
Hit him three – four times.
Laughed Kraljević Marko:
„Oh, champion, black Arab,
Do you joke, or seriously fight?"
Squealed the Arab like a furious snake:
„I don't joke, but seriously fight!"
Thus Marko said:
„And i think that you joke, sad,
But if you seriously fight,
I have a mace as well,
To hit you three – four times,
How much you hit me,
So shall I hit you,
Then we will go on the field,
And begin a duel."
Took Marko his mace,

And struck the black Arab.
He hit him so gently,
He took the head from his shoulders!
Laughed Kraljević Marko:
„Dear God, thank you for everything,
When a man's head falls quickly,
It's like it never stood on him!"
Marko unsheathed his saber,
And struck the Arab's servants,
Decapitated the forty servants,
But left four unharmed,
He left them alive for the truth,
To speak the truth to all,
How it was for the Arab and Marko.
He took the heads from the field,
And buried them nicely,
So no eagles and raves would eat them,
He adorned the field with arab heads.
He took the Arab's treasure,
And the four Arab servants,
Which he did not wish to kill,
Sent them through Kosovo,
Sent them to all four sides,
To shout through Kosovo the servants:
„Where is a girl for marriage,
May she search for a man,
May she marry in her youth,
And where is a hero for marriage,

> May he marry, for a beloved may he search,
> From now on the is no more wedding tax,
> Marko paid all of it!"

The Arab is the chthonic dragon, the ancestor - Veles, who lives below, in the burial mound. He restricts the life, or in this case the wedding ceremonies, for nine years – the nine months of pregnancy. He has forty guardians, which represent the forty weeks of pregnancy, making nine months in total. After nine years (months) Perun – Marko, kills the Arab and his forty servants. The seventy seven decapitated grooms simply indicate that they are the ancestral skull which the child collects at the age of seven, when descending in the burial mound. He takes the Arab's treasure – the object of the grave; his memory; his essence, and saves the maiden – life. Marko is reborn.

The following song „The Wedding of Popović Stojan" has the same structure as „King Marko and Volkašin", with slight differences of course. Because it's more than four pages long, I will present it to you as a tale and include the verses which are valuable for the sake of this research.

Popović Stojan asked the hand of a Latin[5] princess from Mlet, and he was allowed to have her. However, the king told him not to take any Serbs as matchmakers and guests, but take Bulgarians and Greeks instead, since Serbs are drunkards and provocateurs who will start a fight. But the queen secretly told him to bring the Serbs since the Latins (Croats) might plan something against him, and so he did. They went, ate and drank for three days, the queen gifted them and they went on their journey back, taking the princess with them.

---

[5] In the songs all Catholic Christians are called *Latins,* which in this case is used for the Croatians.

The song continues :

„They went well and joyful,
Moving to the hill, to the mountain,
When on the hill, on the mountain,
A hero sat near the wide road,
Wearing wonderful clothing:
All of silver and pure gold,
Something moves above his teeth,
Big as a lamb from half a year,
His buckles shine through his mustache,
Like the mighty sun through the forest,
Yellow are his legs up to his knees,
Brother, they are pure gold,
Near him lies a mace,
Behind his back a killing spear
In his hips a forged saber,
Drinks the hero, red wine,
Served by a forest vila,
With right hand and a golden cup,
And with the left food she gave him."

This giant which crossed the path of the procession, took their golden gifts and asked to have the bride, takes the role of the black Arab, or the three headed dragon (Triglav; Veles) i.e. and as I have shown in my second book "The Sorcerous Spring" in the fairy tales of the South Slavs the giants appear to have the same role as the dragons, which is why very often they too restrain the waters from flowing and cause drought.

*Kraljević Marko & the Giant of the Latins*

He is an avatar of the ancestor, the one restraining life which the child will release and thus reincarnate. This is why he is described as drinking red wine, an avatar of the blood, served by a fairy, an avatar of the placenta, and wearing such beautiful clothing, representing his honour, his memory which Marko will obtain in the following way:

> „Thus came Kraljević Marko
> Leading the horse with the maiden,
> And the hero spoke to him:
> „Give, you Kraljević Marko,
> Give me the horse and the girl,
> Which they gave you there."
> Answered him Marko Kraljević:
> „Brother, giant of the Latins,
> The horse is not mine, and the maiden is someone else's,
> They gifted me with a heavy mace,
> And i shall give it to you."
> The giant would not ask anymore,
> He went to grab the horse,
> To grab the maiden's horse,
> Marko took the heavy mace,
> And noticed the eyes of the Latin,
> Thus he hit with the heavy mace,
> The Latin between his eyes,
> Both of his eyes fell out,
> Marko liked that,
> So he cut the giant's head,
> Took his beautiful clothes,
> And took he the wedding gifts,

Returning them to the matchmakers."

There we have it once more, Marko decapitating the dragon, giant, ancestor, collecting the objects of the grave, and saving the princess. Marko is reborn – the giant's clothes which he takes are simply his own former honour, glory and memory. His divine self. The description of the giant in this song perfectly matches the description of the dead, or those about to die, in other Serbian epic songs, which proves to us that he indeed is a representative of the ancestors. For example, we see that behind the giant is a killing spear, and the verses of the following song entitled "Kraljević Marko and the falcon", describe Marko in the same way:

> "Prince Marko fell ill
> He laid next to the road
> He stuck his spear above his head
> He tied his horse to his spear..."

We see that Marko, knowing that he would die, lies next to the road and stabs his spear behind his head, just like the giant of the previous song. The song "The death of the mother of the Jugović brothers" describes a similar scene:

> "...Dead she finds nine Jugovitch brothers
> And the tenth, the Jug Bogdan, their father.
> Above their heads stuck nine battle-spears....

In both previous songs we find the motif of sticking the battle spear above or behind the head of the dead, or soon to be dead. In the song "The death of the warlord Kaica" we find this motif as well, but also the description of a full tumulus burial:

> "...They buried the warlord Kaica,
> They stuck his spear above his head,
> They tied his horse to his spear,
> They placed his weapons next to him,
> They made tumulus over his body..."

Thus we see how the motif we first encountered in the song „The Wedding of Popović Stojan" is inseparable from how the dead are described in Serbian epic poetry, confirming that the song essentially speaks of reincarnation. Furthermore, what is fascinating about these songs is that they can be archaeologically confirmed.

*Spear "stabbed" into a Scordisci Celtic warrior burial (#11) at Karaburma (Belgrade), Serbia (1st c. BC)*

On this image you see a spearhead stabbed into the grave of a Scordisci Celtic warrior discovered in Serbia. The question is, why do Serbian epic songs describe Iron age Celtic burials in the Balkans? Could it be that the local population was not originally Celtic, but got Celticized, hence why these traditions were preserved is Serbian folklore?

Whatever the case may be, these songs confirm a continuation of the oral tradition among the Serbs since at least the Iron Age, whereas we know that the traditions stem from much further back, in the age of the Neanderthal. Likewise, this is also one of many things which confirm that there is a continuation of culture and traditions among the South Slavs which originates from much before the imagined Slavic "migration" on the Balkans, and that the native population was not Romanized to the degree that we are taught. Archaeology also confirms this, but that's another topic.

Continuing with our wedding songs, in the song called "Dete Golomeše and Krali Marko"[6] the person getting married is Marko, whereas the child acts as his best man escorting the bride. The song is basically the same as „King Marko and Volkašin", but it describes how Marko is preparing for a wedding, yet he does not have a best man, so he finds a naked orphan child living in the sand and dirt, and asks him to be his best man. As we know from before, this child is in fact seven years old, the child participating in the reincarnation ritual. The song begins with the following verses:

> „Went Marko to search for a maiden,
> He traveled across the wide earth,
> He could not choose a girl.
> He passed towns and villages,

---

[6] **Dete Golomeše** simply means "naked child", since *dete* means "child", and *golomeše* translates as "naked belly".

> Nowhere could he find a girl he liked.
> Marko searched for a maiden for him:
> To be beautiful, the most beautiful,
> And that there would be none other like her.
> Popular was the Viluška maiden,
> From the Latin land.
> The tsar had nine sons,
> Only one daughter – a virgin,
> Kept for nine years under a veil
> Not to be burned by the bright sun,
> Neither by the sun, nor the moon."

This is a very obvious symbolism of the foetus being in the womb for nine months, untouched neither by the light of the sun, nor the moon. Marko asked for her hand, he gathered his matchmakers, but he did not have a best man. When he found the poor orphan in the sand and asked him to be his best man, the child said to Marko:

> „How can I be your best man,
> When I am naked like this?"
> And Marko answered him:
> „Marko has clothes to give you,
> Marko has a sword to give you,
> Marko has a horse to give you."
> Then the child agreed,
> Took him Marko Kraljević
> Took him to his courtyard,
> Took him to the white garments.
> He chose the best garments,

> Which Marko never wore in vain,
> He wore it once a year,
> Only once, for Easter.
> He took him to pick a horse -
> He chose the piebald one,
> Which Marko never rode in vain,
> He rode it only when going in battle,
> In battle with the black Arab.
> He took him to pick a sword,
> He chose Marko's sword,
> Which can be folded twelve times,
> Which cuts wood and stone,
> Which Marko never used in vain,
> He used it only when going in battle,
> In battle with the black Arab.
> Adorned, Marko Kraljević
> Adorned he three hundred matchmakers,
> Adorned he the witness and second witness,
> Thus off they went to the maiden's courtyard,
> Ahead rode the young best man.

So we see here that the child literally becomes Marko by dressing up as him, and not just in any clothes, but clothes worn only for Easter – the spring equinox, the end of winter and beginning of spring, the end of the first pregnancy and the beginning of the second. And he does not take any horse or sword, but the ones used only in battle against the black Arab, which we know by now to be the chthonic dragon. Therefore the child becomes Marko, and as such he defeats the black Arab, thus saving the princess – the life – and being successfully reborn. We see this in the following verses:

Overtook them, the black Arab,
From afar turned their heads:
„I have set laws and orders:
Here a maiden will not pass,
All of you will pass by me,
And everyone will leave the gifts!"
And everyone passed,
Everyone left the gifts.
In the back stood the young best man,
Thus spoke to him the black Arab:
„Now you, little best man,
Let's see what you shall gift me!"
The best man softly answered:
When i went from mother's courtyard,
I swore to the maiden's mother,
Swore to protect the bride,
To protect her from the evils on the road,
I give my head, the bride I don't give!"
The black Arab became furious,
He took his heavy mace,
To hit the child,
And to the child he said:
„Stand your ground, I will aim and hit!"
The child stood his ground,
His horse was heroic,
**Nine** times in battle he went,
First he saw the mace
And rose up higher,

> The Arab aimed at the child's chest,
> And he threw the heavy mace,
> The horse kneeled,
> The mace missed him,
> The Arab thus spoke:
> „Don't move, may God kill you!"
> And the child answered him:
> „I am born from a mother once,
> And I wish to fight you.
> Stand your ground, I shall throw!"
> The Arab stood his ground,
> The child threw the heavy mace,
> And hit the black Arab,
> **Nine** elbows underground it drove him.
> Thus he gathered the gifts,
> And took him to Marko's courtyard.

The very fact that a child appears as a hero and slays a dragon / Arab, especially when he appears to be seven years old, is enough to show even to the most determined skeptic that our myths and tales essentially describe the process of reincarnation. And that what Marie Cachet explained in her book „The Secret Of The She-Bear", and myself in my previous books, is indeed true.

However, some wedding songs do not speak of three headed dragons or Arabs, but instead they speak of masks with which the matchmakers were supposed to be chased away. For example, in the song called „The Wedding Of Crnojević Ivo" which we find in the oldest document of Serbian epic poetry, the „Erlangen Manuscript", upon the orders of the king, the Arab does the following:

> „With difficulty the Arab took that,
> And went he in the green forest,
> Where the roads of the matchmakers are,
> There he sat in ambush,
> He put on three heads,
> And on his back skin of wolf,
> When the matchmakers arrived,
> Then the Arab came out on the road.
> From his mouth fire burns,
> From his forehead thunder strikes,
> And from his nose a terrible rain comes -
> The whole black hill was covered in fog."

As always, Marko decapitates the Arab and saves the princess. In another song called „The Wedding Of Yanko Of Sibiu" we don't find an Arab or a three headed mask, but instead a very primitive and essentially animistic disguise:

> „Nothing could stop Lazanka Planinka,
> Thus he dressed in wolf's skin,
> And he put a bear's skin,
> And he went after them."

Here we have the most archaic appearance of Veles, as a wolf and/or a bear. He is the one who gives wealth, prosperity and abundance, but also the one who restrains it. The fact that the songs describe such disguises also implies the possibility that in the past there was a ritual which occurred during the weddings where the chthonic deity would be slain for his attempt to stop the wedding, whereas the engaged couple would represent a divine couple, deities ready to be married.

The bear is the oldest ancestral animal of all Europeans, but the wolf is not less important in that role. Especially among the Serbs and other South Slavs the wolf was regarded as a totemic ancestor, whereas the title of a „wolf herdsman" among all Slavs is given to Veles. The wolf, like the bear, despite representing the sum of the ancestors also represents the female reproductive system, or simply the mother. This is also evident in the Serbian traditions after a baby is born, where the father would open the house door, stand on the doorstep and announce the birth of his son by saying "Rodila vučica vuka!" (A she-wolf gave birth to a wolf cub!). And the mother would announce its wolf nature by singing a lullaby to the child which started with "Nini sine, vuče I bauče, vučica te u gori rodila" (Sleep my son, my wolf, a she-wolf gave birth to you in a mountain).

To ensure the health of children after being born, but also after performing healing rituals on an ill person, the baby, or the person would be pulled through the skin from a wolf's jaw, or the entire jaw. This was done as imitative magic, symbolically representing the person's rebirth as a healthy individual.

Marko also is described as wearing a wolf or bear cloak and a cap of wolf skin, but this does not make him a representative of the chthonic deity. It simply means that Marko is *in* the mother's womb. He is the child which is going to be reborn, as demonstrated many times by now. It is also a refference to the pre-historic European understanding that by wearing an animal's skin one inherits its power. Therefore if the wolf and bear are the primordial animistic representatives of the ancestral sum, then killing them, eating parts of their body, wearing pendants made of bones or their skin as a cloak meant that symbolically one inherits the life force of the ancestors. In other words he becomes them - he is reborn. This explains why Vuk („wolf") is a very common name among Serbs, but also Vukašin like Marko's father, whose name means "wolf's son".

These heroic wedding songs definitely have been altered through time, and we can not know, at least not at the moment, if they stem from a deeper Proto-Slavic root or represent a local South Slavic development throughout the ages. If we were to examine that topic we would have to search for such songs and motifs in the folklore of all three Slavic groups, compare them and reconstuct a myth based on the elements which they have in common. Unfortunately nobody has undertaken this task yet, but the Croatian author Radoslav Katičić undertook a similar task and was able to reconstruct a mythological song about the Slavic god Jarilo, by examining the songs sang for St. George's day in all three Slavic groups, and also legends related to him. In the song we don't find the same pattern which appears in these heroic South Slavic songs, but we can recognize some similar elements:

> Jarilo walked a long road,
> Burdensome was his wander,
> As a foreigner he appeared,
> Over a bridge, cracking and trembling,
> His right foot leaked water,
> Muddy to the knee,
> Wet up to his shoulders,
> His left foot was ablaze, sparking,
> The path was dry and dusty.
> Jarilo came from beyond the meadow green,
> From beyond the bloody red sea,
> Bringing health and well being,
> His shoes were torn from the long road
> Came he from the green meadow,
> Wherever he stepped, the field gave birth,
> The black forest turned green,

The valley and the hill,

Yet every mother wept in sorrow,

For her daughter dear,

Who she had to offer to the serpent.

In the cave amid the sea,

When the serpent showed itself,

Jarilo rode towards it,

Noble blooded Jarilo,

First among heroes,

Pulled out his shining sword,

And cut off the serpent's head.

When the serpent fell dead,

The maidens gathered around,

The music began to play,

They began to dance.

A cuckoo sang early in the morning,

In the meadow green,

In the meadow green, on a dry bough,

On a dry bough, on a purple willow,

On a purple willow, on a tall pine,

Above the cold waters.

It was not a cuckoo, but a young bride,

All the maidens married,

Only Mara remained,

She walked through the town,

And woke her brothers in law:

"Rise my nine brothers in law,

Nine brothers in law, brothers of mine,

Jarilo has arrived in the meadow green,
In the meadow green, on the dry bough."
Mara had a golden apple,
Which many men wanted to possess.
To whom the apple, to him the maiden!
To Jarilo the apple, to Jarilo the maiden!
Jarilo had now an apple of gold,
Which in the wide field he rolled,
In the wide field, in the dark forest,
In the dark forest, in her maidenhood!"

This song is obviously an ancient myth, and I won't go into detail by explaining its symbols and meaning, since I have previously done that in my second book "The Sorcerous spring", but you are welcome to do it yourself. Also, the song does not resemble the pattern of the South Slavic epic wedding songs, but it was important to include this song because we see that even here Veles (the dragon) appears as somebody obstructing the wedding of Jarilo and Mara, for which he is killed. Therefore the motif we are dealing with in the wedding songs is obviously ancient, and it is purely mythological.

# V
## Marko's Engagement

Marko heard that the tsar from over the sea had a daughter for marriage, so he asked for her hand. The tsar promised her, but he asked of Marko to catch and kill the mountain lion. Marko dressed in lion skin and went to the mountain. He roared like a wounded lion and attracted several lions to him, so he killed not one, but five of them. The tsar was impressed by Marko's courage, so he asked of him to kill the dragon (aždaja) who lives in the cave and eats one child per day. Marko shaved and disguised himself as a maiden by putting on female clothes, so he went to the entrance of the cave where the dragon lived. When the dragon appeared he killed it, cut its head off and took it to the tsar, making the whole kingdom very happy. Then the tsar gave his daughter to Marko, but under the condition that he carries her on his back while he swims across the sea. Marko swam three days and nights, and on the fourth day he saw land, which made him joyful. However, when he was near the shore, some kind of ugly sea fish ate the princess, so he went out alone.

**Meaning**

Personally, this tale reminds me of the myth of the twelve labours of Heracles, except that Marko has to pass three labours before he is reborn, which of course represent the three pregnancy cycles. The princess Marko wants to marry lives beyond the sea i.e. she is from the womb, as the sea is the amniotic water of the womb. Marko's first task is to kill a mountain lion, so he dresses in lion skin. This reminds us of Heracles who also dresses with the skin of the lion which he kills. In essence it is linked to the primordial hunter gatherer tradition that by dressing up as the killed animal one obtains its power. Of course this is the most animistic way to become the Gods/ancestors, as these animals usually represented the ancestral sum.

Same is the case for the lion, who is an avatar of the maternal side of the placenta, the side which devours the body of the mother, so to speak. Therefore Marko's victory over the lion(s) represents the cutting of the umbilical cord and the end of the first pregnancy.

His second challenge is to kill a dragon living in the depths of a cave. A very obvious symbolism, as the cave is the womb, the dragon is the ancestor, the umbilical cord. Its decapitation represents the cutting of the umbilical cord and the successful rebirth of the child. Another thing which tells us that this really is an explanation of the pregnancy is that Marko disguises himself in female clothing before descending into the dragon's cave. This is because in the early stage of the development of the foetus, it is neither male nor female, but androgynous, so to speak. This puts Marko in direct relation to Thor who in the poem *Þrymskviða* has to dress up as the Goddess Freyja in order to descend into the home of the Ettins and take his hammer back. His hammer is of course the heart, life itself, meaning that Thor dresses up as a female in order to be reborn, exactly the same as Marko.

This motif also appears in ancient Greece where Heracles dressed up as a woman serves Omphale, the queen of Lydia. The name of the queen Omphale is derived from "omphalos", meaning navel, and this connection has never been made clear. But when we know that the myth is about reincarnation, and that Heracles is the foetus, the reason why the name of the person he serves means "navel" is very obvious.

These motifs are used by the Liberals today as "proof" that we Europeans have traditionally practiced homosexuality and cross-dressing, and use them to promote their degenerate sexuality. This is of course completely wrong, since as described before, the only reason these motifs exist is symbolic, and they represent a certain stage of the reincarnation process.

After killing the dragon Marko marries the princess, he is reunited with the ancestral spirit, but in the end he arrives to the shore alone after swimming for three days and nights. This is simply because the foetus is born alone, arriving from "beyond the sea" which is the amniotic fluid of the womb, whilst the three days and nights are a symbolic way to say that he passed the three cycles of pregnancy.

# VI
## Prince Marko & Philip The Magyar

I will tell you what I have heard from the old ones. When the old ones gathered for some feasts, some dinners, some celebrations, they told some tales about Krali Marko, some tales, some songs. From them I remember only one.

Once upon a time Krali Marko was traveling across the world. He left his wife and son at home, and Philip the Magyar took advantage of his absence. He took his wife, he took his son, he stole his weapons and he hid in his castle. His castle was so big that it was surrounded by seven walls. When Marko returned home and saw that his wife, son and possessions had been taken, he went to search for Philip the Magyar. Philip was so hidden in his castle that Marko could not jump over the walls. He tried and tried but always fell somewhere between. So he went back to his castle and waited for three years.

After three years Philip the Magyar thought that Marko wouldn't be coming back anymore, so he opened the gates of his seven walls. He went out and thought that there was no threat anymore, so he let everyone be free to come in and out of his yard, even his home. Meanwhile, a son was born to him so they decided to have a celebration, invited friends and other guests. Among these guests was Krali Marko. He disguised himself as a beggar so well that even his wife and son could not recognize him. Therefore, he wasn't as he was before.

On the celebration they ate and drank a lot. They took Marko's cup, and everyone was trying to drink a full cup of wine, but nobody could. In the end, the son of Marko tried, how old he was I don't know, but managed to drink the full cup. His mother hit him and said "You will be like your father, drinking a full cup!" They took his sword and tried to unsheathe it, but nobody managed to do it except the boy, his son. So his mother hit him and told him not to be like his father.

In the end the disguised Marko asked to try if he could unsheathe his sword, and when he had it out, he cut the heads off of all the enemies that were there, including of course Philip the Magyar.

Then he asked his wife "Do you want to serve me with wine and brandy, or do you want to hold the light for me while I drink?" this was supposed to be her punishment for betraying him. The wife answered "I shall hold the light for you", so he poured oil on her, wrapped her in a rug and burned her alive.

## Meaning

This is a fairly simple story to understand. Philip the Magyar replaces the ancient chthonic deity Veles – the ancestor. He steals the wife, son and possessions of Marko, possibly Perun.

The castle of Philip is an image of the womb, but also the burial mound where the life (Marko's son and wife) and ancestral possessions (Marko's cup and weapon) are kept. It is impenetrable, unless the child participating in the reincarnation ritual is at least seven years old, which is what the seven walls around it stand for. This is why Marko – the child, is unable to pass them. He is not yet of age. When he is of age he is able to enter into Philip's home but only under a disguise. This describes once again the only way the children were able to gain access into the realm of the dead – by putting a disguise, a mask, usually covering themselves with animal skins, skulls, bones, horns, feathers, and covering their faces with ash or soot. By doing this they symbolically died, because only the dead have access to the underworld, and covering oneself with ash or soot was the simplest way of doing this. Therefore Marko is the child entering the underworld to retrieve what is his i.e. to be reborn.

When inside the underworld – in the home of Philip the Magyar, Marko notices that everybody tries to unsheathe his sword and drink from his cup, but nobody is able to succeed. Of course, since the items belong to Marko. He is the only one who can reincarnate. This is why the only one able to drink the wine and unsheathe the sword is his son – Marko himself, the child in the depths of the burial mound.

The unsheathing of the sword is essentially the same motif as that of the Arthurian legend, where the sword stuck in the stone can only be taken out by the child Arthur. Here this is the son of Marko i.e. Marko himself, reincarnated, whilst the sword stands for the umbilical cord. He drinks the wine in a cup, avatar of the placenta, while the wine is an avatar of the blood, and it is the sacred drink of immortality, or wisdom, which appears in all European mythologies. This symbolism can also be found with mead, normal water or sometimes golden water. This implies the possibility that upon entering in the burial mound where the children met the sorcerer impersonating the chthonic deity, alcohol was used to produce an altered state of consciousness. And by that I don't mean psychedelic alteration, but a drunken one, as the state of being drunk and unable to function normally is close, symbolically, to the state of being dead. In the earliest form of this reincarnation ritual this was probably just fermented fruit.

Marko decapitated Philip – the child takes the ancestral skull from the burial mound; the umbilical cord is cut. Marko is reborn.

The burning of his wife could hint towards the flame being kindled in the burial mound, symbolizing his rebirth. But it could also be related to the burning of the effigy of the Goddess Mara/Morana, because in some songs the person being burned is named Mara, the tavern maiden.

# VII
## PRINCE MARKO & THE DUKAGJIN CHILD

A very interesting and unusual motif which appears in the cycle of epic songs about Kraljević Marko is his battle with a seven year old child who is said to be a greater hero than him. Now how is it possible that a seven year old child is stronger than Marko, the giant and proud hero? Well, let's find out:

> Walked around King Marko,
> Walked across the Kosovo plain,
> He noticed the evening star,
> Thus Marko spoke to the star:
> „Oh, you star, evening star,
> You stand high, you see far,
> Is there a hero greater than me?"
> Spoke to him the evening star:
> „Oh Marko from Varoš town,
>  You are Marko, a golden hero,
> But what is the Dukagjin[7] child,
> Young, of six – seven years
> A marble slab with his right hand,
> He turns over his shoulder -
> He will be a hero above heroes!"
> Took Marko from Varoš,
> Took his mighty steed,
> Rode he across the roads,

---
[7] Dukagjin (Serbian: Дукађин) is a mountainous region in the northern part of modern day Albania. It was part of the Serbian Empire before the Ottoman occupation.

He wend to Dukad town,

He cursed the Dukagjin Child,

Whose house was very noticable:

His fort is made of iron,

His gates made of iron sheet,

In his yard a tall maple tree,

Upon which heads hang!

Arrived Marko and shouted:

„Oh you child, Dukagjin child,

„I come to be your guest,

I shall take you as a blood-brother!"

That he heard, the Dukagjin Child,

Thus he spoke, he answered:

Away with you, unknown hero,

Or I shall throw you from my tall roof!"

His mother thus told him:

„Oh son, Child of Dukagjin,

Why kill a man for no reason,

He maybe comes to be our guest?"

They opened the iron gates,

Opened them, Marko entered,

They began eating and drinking,

Ate and drank three days and nights!

Thus spoke Krale Marko:

„Dukagjin Child, lovely blood-brother,

Let's go for a walk,

Ride through the green fields,

To walk the horses for a while!"

Damn him, Marko the trickster,

He lied to the Dukagjin Child,

He took him to the green fields!

When they were in the green field,

Marko spoke to the child:

„Let's try ourselves, child,

Try ourselves with our heroic arms!"

A greater was, the Dukagjin Child,

A greater was he a hero than Marko,

He grabbed him, but he moved back!

„Stand your ground, Dukagjin Child!"

„Oh Marko, dear blood-brother,

I have not with me my mighty weapons,

I left half of it at home."

Thus spoke Marko the trickster:

„Let's try ourselves, child!"

He did not let him go,

Made him duel with their arms, -

They grabbed themselves from afar.

But the child, the Dukagjin Child,

Was still very young,

Young, of seven years!

Marko threw his yellow[8] mace,

And hit the Dukagjin Child,

Hit him right in the forehead.

---

[8] The original word in the song is *жолта*, meaning "yellow". However, this is just a symbolic way to say "golden", since the Proto-Slavic *žьltъ* – "yellow" is a variation of *zoltъ* – "golden", derived from the PIE root *$ǵʰelh_3$-* ("yellow; to shine")

>Thus spoke the Dukagjin Child:
>"Damn your soul, old mother,
>You betrayed me to Kraljević Marko."

## Meaning

Since there are different versions of this song, it's good to mention that in one version Marko loses the battle to the Dukagjin Child, but it makes no difference in what the meaning of the songs is. In a third version the battle ends without a winner because they realize that Marko is the child's uncle, but even here the meaning of the tale is not lost, because the end is a moment of self-realization i.e. awakening to who one really is. In this third version the child's clothes are described as decorated with gold and precious stones, whilst on his head he has twelve feathers attached to nine silver plates. These numbers are of course symbolic, as the whole tale of Marko's battle with a seven year old child.

Marko and the Dukagjin child are the same individual split in two, and their battle simply represents the reincarnation of the ancestor in the body of the seven year old child. This is why the child's clothes are so rich – it's the shining honour, spirit and memory of the ancestor. His nine silver plates stand for the nine months of pregnancy, while his twelve feathers stand for the twelve months of the year. It is the time passed, the cycle of three pregnancies within the year which are concluded on the 12th month of the year, when the child dies and is reborn – the winter solstice.

The child's fort is made of iron, which alludes to the impenetrable nature of the womb/ grave, unless the child is of age, and in the yard is a tall tree on which decapitated heads hang. This of course tries to tell us that the Dukagjin Child claimed the heads of many heroes, but in essence it represents the collected ancestral heads of his previous lives, hanging on the tree – the sum of the ancestors. Marko is of age, he is allowed to enter into the home (underworld) thanks to the mother, which in this case acts as the deity of the underworld – Vela, the midwife, the great She-Bear who chooses the one to be reborn. There they eat and drink for three days and nights, which represents the child nourished within the womb – the drink of immortality previously explained.

The green fields where they duel should also be understood as the underworld (the womb), as in the Slavic mythology the realm of Veles, the place where the dead spirits were said to go when traveling beyond the great stream (amniotic fluid; milky way) was imagined as an evergreen place with vast valleys and forests. There Marko throws his golden mace and hits the child onto the forehead, thus killing him. Gold symbolically is honour, glory, but also blood – the blood the baby is nourished with, by the umbilical cord. The forehead has a special symbolism which we haven't met so far. It is the seat of the so called "third eye" or "spiritual eye", for just as the baby is nourished through the biological navel whilst in the womb of the mother, so the seven year old child is nourished, or rather enlightened to his true nature through this navel of wisdom. Hence why the mace is golden. Marko defeats the seven year old Dukagjin Child, he becomes the hero above all heroes – he is reborn. If the child defeated Marko, as it happens in the other version, it wouldn't make any difference – the seven year old child defeats the ancestor i.e. he is reborn.

# VIII
## THE DERVISH CHILD & MARKO

A little child was stolen,
Stolen from its golden cradle,
Stolen by three naked dervishes,
And taken to the dervish land.
There the child grew,
And grew a mighty hero at his ninth year.
Then the naked dervishes said:
„Come on, child, go away,
Go back to your,
To your peaceful land!
Thus they put a dervish gun in his hand,
And a dervish robe on his shoulder,
And told him: - Go away,
Go away to your peaceful land,
Your father is Kraljević Marko,
Your mother is the young Markoitsa![9]
Stood up the little naked dervish,
Became a beggar in front of mosques,
From one mosque to another,
From one tekije[10] to another he begged,
In Turkish he swore, as an infidel he prayed:
„Oh God, dear God!

---
[9] Among the South Slavs the wife is usually called after her husband's name. In this case Marko is the husband, so his wife is Markoitsa, meaning "Marko's (wife)".
[10] Tekije is a sacral building used only by Sufi Muslims.

Shall I ever find my peaceful land,

My father, Kraljević Marko,

My mother, young Markoitsa?"

Came the child in the middle of the road,

On the road he found cold water,

Cold water, two deep shades,

He drank water, under the shade he sat,

and to god he prayed:

(*The same prayer as above is repeated.*)

There, where the young dervish sat,

There, where he sat and prayed,

Appeared a good hero,

Carrying a bloody saber.

Then spoke the good hero,

The good hero, Krale Marko:

„Oh God, dear God!

I traveled nine years through the dervish land,

Searching everywhere for the dervishes,

But, they were on the ground!"

The good hero went under the shade,

And said to the young naked dervish:

„Hey, child, you naked dervish!

Why do you sit and weep?"

Then the little dervish spoke:

„Hey, hero, unkown hero!

I search for my peaceful land,

My father Marko,

My mother, young Markoitsa!"

When Kraljević Marko heard that,
To the young dervish he said:
„Come, let's fight a bit,
To see who is a greater hero."
The young dervish agreed,
They went to duel, to fight,
When they grabbed each other,
From morning until midday,
Neither the hero, nor the dervish fell.
Thus spoke Kraljević Marko:
„I traveled nine years through the dervish land,
Nowhere did I find a hero like you!
Thus said the young dervish:
„I am Marko's child, Yankula.
They stole me from a golden cradle,
Stole me the three naked dervishes,
Took me to the dervish land.
There I grew nine years,
Now they released me,
To go to my peaceful land,
They gave me a gun in the hands,
They gave me a robe on the side.

*( He continues to explain how he begged and prayed, the same way as described before. )*

Thus spoke Marko:
„It's you, Yankula child!"

He hugged and kissed him and said:
„So long I traveled across the dervish land,
All the dervishes I fought,
Like you nowhere did I find!"
Then Marko took him,
Threw him on his horse,
Took him to his home,
And called the young Markovitsa:
„Come, Markovitsa, to see our Yankula!"

## Meaning

This song is very simple and obvious, but unfortunately completely changed from its original form as a myth. Yes, this song reeks of Ottoman influence, but its essence is not lost, and this is what we are here for – to remove the foreign influence of our songs, and reveal and understand their purely European, that is to say *pagan* essence.

It's very simple – Marko and the child are the same individual searching for himself. The ancestor and the body of the child in which he will reincarnate. The nine years are, as always the nine months of pregnancy before the child is (re)born. Here the underworld, the womb, the realm of the dead, the burial mound is what they call „dervish land", and the three headed dragon, Triglav – the chthonic God, the ancestor who steals the life (baby) from the cradle is represented as the three naked dervishes, same as when the black Arab replaced the three headed beast. Marko and the child met under the shade of the tree, the sacred tree that is, and the sacred well underneath it.

This is where the child sat and drank, just as the foetus sits near the placenta and „drinks" from the blood. When Marko appeared they engaged in a battle, naturally since there is always a battle between the ancestor and the offspring.

When experiencing the child's strength Marko is convinced that it really is his son i.e he is the real person to be reincarnated. They recognize each other. The individual finds himself back – Marko is reborn.

# IX
## THE CAPTIVITY OF KRALJEVIĆ MARKO

Yesterday Marko got married,
When the white day dawned,
Then Marko to hunt went,
To hunt, in a distant land,
A distant land, at the Turkish town.
The hero grew tired on the road,
He rested under the green fir,
There came three young Turkish maidens,
They took Marko in his sleep,
They put him in deep darkness,
Behind nine keys they locked him.
He whined and cried, tied up in the dark,
His face he wounded with his hand,
With the blood he wrote a letter,
He sent it to his beloved,
To his beloved, or to his mother,
But on the window his beloved was,
Upon the letter's arrival,
With a sad voice she smiled,
Thus wrote to Marko's mother:

*(She explains Marko's situation using the same verses from above, from verse 1 to 17.)*

When the mother understood her words,
She answered nicely:

„Blessed be, young bride,

God would help you,

My sorrow would buy Marko's freedom."

Then the young bride answered:

„Do not despair, mother of mine,

But send the youngest servant,

To fetch my black steed,

Of which Marko is unaware,

And sew me a priest's garment,

Whilst I tie my hair like a man."

The mother did as she was told,

She saddled her horse.

Then she mounted the horse,

And rode it swiftly,

Galloping towards the Turkish forests,

And she saw the three young maidens,

In God's name she called them:

„Blessed be, three young Turkish maidens!"

They answered nicely:

„Blessed be, unknown hero."

„Today I make nine years,

To travel as a hero from town to town,

Every town gave me three prisoners,

I don't ask for more than one."

Thus the maidens spoke:

„Blessed be unknown hero,

Which prisoner do you ask us to give?"

And she answered politely:

„I ask you for Kraljević Marko."
They gave her Kraljević Marko,
She rode forth with her horse…

The song continues to describe how Marko begged her to release him while she rode, but she makes him believe that she will throw him in the dungeon of her castle. In the end they arrive home, she releases him and Marko grabs his saber, but she presents herself: „This is your beloved, with her you were and spoke, but you did not recognize her, hero."

## Meaning

Here we have the classic mytheme of the princess being held captive by the three headed dragon, and in the end rescued by the hero, only the roles in this song are changed and Marko is the one being rescued by his beloved. In this song we have a similar situation as the one described before, only this time the role of the three naked dervishes is taken by three Turkish maidens. These are again the three fairies, midwives or Fates if you will, just another aspect of the thrice ancestral deity which can appear as masculine or feminine. Everything which was associated with chthonic ancestral spirits, deities or creatures was transformed into Turks, Arabs, Dervishes or even Jews during the Ottoman period of the Haemus peninsula.

In the beginning we see that Marko goes hunting, which implies that he is searching for himself, to be reborn. That's why he goes to a distant land, to the Turkish town. The distant land or even more precisely the Turkish town represents the realm of the dead. It is the previously mentioned Trojan town (cf. Troy; Labyrinth; womb) where the God Trojan - Veles ("thrice") lives, in this song represented by the three Turkish maidens.

After a while Marko decides to rest and sleep under a fir tree, which is a metaphor for the foetus attached to the placenta, but also the dead ancestor in the burial mound. Traditionally trees which grew above the burial mound, as well as the other plants, were considered to be most sacred. They were not cut, nor were their fallen branches gathered or their fruit harvested. Thus the dead literally rest beneath them. This was the first form of a temple in Europe, a fenced area which was completely left to Mother Nature.

Marko is tied up by the three maidens (Trigla; the three headed dragon) and locked away in the darkness, behind nine locks – he is the ancestor in the underworld / womb, whilst the nine locks are simply the nine months of pregnancy. In order for his beloved – the child participating in the reincarnation ritual - to enter the realm of the dead – the Turkish forest - she first must impersonate the dead. Thus she disguises herself, wearing priest's robe, which in Orthodox Christianity is black, and she rides a black horse. The horse is also a very common symbol of the placenta. The nine years which she said that she travelled are again the nine months of pregnancy, of course, since she and Marko are the same individual split in two. Marko recognizes her, he is reborn.

# X
## PRINCE MARKO AND THE BLACK ARAB

Marko went to the wide Skopje,
To see the churches and monasteries,
Are they all standing upright,
And the tall towers above Skopje.
There sat the young Markovitsa,
On the couch, knitting socks,
Came to her the fogs and mists,
It was the Ala, the Ala
*The Ala, the black Arab.*
Thus spoke young Markovitsa:
„Dear God, Marko is not here,
What is that which is coming?"
She did not finish her words,
A loud knocking was on the door,
The black Arab arrived,
Young Markovitsa was terrified,
She trembled with fear,
She dropped the socks and needle,
Uttered the black Arab,
Spoke the black Arab:
„Are you here Marko, come out,
To measure our heroic strength?"
Answered the young Markovitsa:
„Go away black Arab,
Marko is not at home,

If he comes he will take your head!"
The black Arab became furious,
The black Arab became enraged,
So he broke the door down,
Grabbed the young Markovitsa,
Put her on the horse in front of him,
And rode to the field of Tikveš.
What was the fairy Vela,
She was Marko's blood-sister,
News she sent to him:
„Where are you Marko, my good blood-brother,
Hurry and come back quickly,
The Arab grabbed your first loved,
Took her to the flat roads."
The news reached him quickly,
Quickly Marko returned,
And crossed the black Arab,
Crossed him in the Tikveš field.
On a meeting stood Marko the hero,
Thus spoke to the Ala,
Thus spoke to the black Arab:
„Stand your ground black Arab,
Aren't the Arab maidens enough?
Aren't the Egyptian maidens enough?
That you come to the town of Prilep,
And steal my young Markovitsa!"
Answered the black Arab:
Stand your ground, infidel Marko,

To measure our strength,
To see who is a greater champion!"
Stood Marko his ground,
Aimed the black Arab,
Aimed with his heavy mace.
Yet Marko's horse,
The horse kneeled, the mace missed,
Thus spoke the black Arab:
„Stand still Marko, I will throw once more,
Because that was cheating!"
Answered Marko, the good hero:
„Hold on, Arab, hold on, black dog,
To see who is the hero Marko,
Glorified across the wide earth!"
Dear God, a mighty fight began!
The horses screaming across the Tikveš field,
The sabers clashing, maces striking.
The battle lasted three days and nights:
Stood the bright moon,
Stood those bright stars,
To behold a battle unseen before,
Which never happened in the world.
Thus spoke Marko the good hero:
„Come down, Arab, come down, black dog,
To fight with our hands!
Both came down to fight,
On one side champions fought,
On the other the horses fought,

Šarko's[11] hoofs deep in the earth,
The Arab horse deep to the knees.
The Arab horse spewed white foam,
Marko's horse spewed fire.
What was the black Arab,
Was down in the earth to his knees,
The good hero was down to his waist.
The battle lasted,
Marko lost his strength.
Thus shouted Marko the good hero:
„Where are you, dear fairy Vela,
Where are you, my dear blood-sister,
Where are you, to help me,
For I have lost my strength!"
Vela the fairy appeared,
With a long white dress,
She spoke to Marko the good hero:
„Listen Marko, listen, good hero,
Should I teach you that as well?
Search in your blonde hair,
Take out your hidden knife,
Cut his lungs out,
There lie nine fierce snakes,
Eight sleep, only one is awake,
And you crush their heads,
Then the Arab will fall!"
Thus Marko his knife took,

---

[11] Šarko, Šaran, Šarac or other variations is the name of Marko's horse, and his name means "patterned; piebald."

Cut out the Arab's lungs,
He killed the nine fierce snakes,
Killed the snakes, the Arab fell.
He cut the Arab's head off,
He is the hero above all heroes,
He defeated that terrible force,
Terrible force, the black Arab.
The sun rose smiling,
The farmers sang in the fields,
The shepherds played their kavals,
Maidens and brides sang.
All together in great joy!
There is no more black Arab,
No more of that greasy dog!

## Meaning

In this song the black Arab is clearly referred to as *Ala*, thus confirming once again that his role was firstly taken by the dragon, or more precisely Veles. He is the ancestor who steals the life away from Marko. Marko and his wife are the individual split in two, with her representing the life which Marko needs to release. The nine snakes living within him are a symbol of the umbilical cord, but also the nine months of pregnancy. Marko is unable to kill the Arab so he asks the help of his fairy blood-sister, which is an ancestral spirit - his accumulated honour expressed as a guardian spirit. Her name is Vela, just like the previously mentioned Goddess who I said is essentially a midwife, of the body and the mind. And indeed she appears as a midwife who instructs Marko how to be (re)born. Naturally in order for the child to be reborn the womb must be opened after the nine months of pregnancy, and the umbilical cord to be cut. This is described as the opening of the Arab, killing the nine snakes and decapitating him.

Marko & the Black Arab

# XI
## King Marko & the Yellow Merchant

Gained power the yellow Merchant,[12]

Gained power in Solun[13] town:

He killed seventy kings,

And executed eighty bans,[14]

He built nine towers,

Nine towers from heroic heads!

He walked, the yellow Merchant,

He walked across the white towers,

He walked and he spoke:

„Why don't I have a dear mother,

To sit in my colourful towers?

Why don't I have a dear sister,

To clean these white towers?

Why don't I have a lovely bride,

To walk around these colourful towers?"

This he said, this he spoke,

He remembered, God may kill him,

That there is in the town of Prilep,

One hero called king Marko:

Marko has, Marko the leader,

Marko has an old mother,

Marko has a dear sister,

---

[12] In the South Slavic folklore the Yellow Merchant is a synonym for Jew.
[13] Solun is the South Slavic name for Thessaloniki
[14] Ban was a noble title used in several states in Central and Southeast Europe between the VII and XX centuries.

Marko has a lovely bride!
So he sent him a letter:
„Oh Marko, warleader Marko,
Will you, hero, come to me,
Or you will wait for me there,
To see your strength?"
When he received the letter,
Marko became enraged,
But more so he became sad!
He asked his old mother:
„Oh mother, my old mother,
Damn him, may God kill him,
Damn him, the yellow Merchant,
The yellow Merchant from Solun!
For he sent me a letter,
And in it, mother, it is written:
'Oh Marko, warleader Marko,
Will you, hero, come to me,
Or you will wait for me there,
To see your strength?'
Even if he is a greater champion,
Who killed seventy kings,
And eighty bans,
I don't allow him to come here,
I don't allow him to be praised
To be praised as a hero above all,
I shall go to him in Solun town!"
Answered Marko's mother:

„Oh Marko, Marko my dear son,

He is much stronger than you!

You spoke right, you said correctly,

Do not wait for him here, my son,

But there, go there,

Seek him out and find his end!

Disguise yourself as God's beggar,

Dress your fighting horse,

Dress him in a black disguise,

Dress as a beggar of God,

And go to the city of Solun!

There is a white fountain,

A fountain with nine taps,

There goes the yellow Merchant,

Every morning, to drink water,

To wash those yellow feet.

His horse he rides, he rides,

When he arrives, he dismounts his horse,

He kneels to drink water,

Then make sure to cut him with your saber!

But don't cut him in half, son,

Not with the sharp saber,

The saber won't cut him there,

For he has a heart of stone,

Because he drinks that water,

Drinks it with a hungry heart,[15]

---

[15] To do something "with a hungry heart" is the South Slavic equivalent of doing something "with an empty stomach".

Cut his legs at his knees,

Mount your war horse,

Run as much as you can,

So he does not catch you and kill you."

As his mother taught him,

So Marko did and listened:

He dressed his war horse,

He dressed him in a black garment,

He disguised as God's beggar,

He took his saber,

Which he hid in his horse (under its mane),

Here and there across the white roads,

He arrived in the town of Solun.

There he found the white fountain,

He went before sunrise,

When the sun rose, when it shined,

He released his horse to graze,

And sat near the fountain .

A little time had passed,

There he comes from Solun,

There comes, the yellow Merchant,

Riding his horse.

He arrived at the white fountain,

He saw Marko the trickster:

„Good morning, God's beggar!"

„May God give wellness, champion of champions!"

He dismounted his fast horse,

He drank from the eight taps,

He kneeled to the ninth,
He kneeled to drink water.
Then Marko, warlord Marko,
Took out his saber,
Struck once, cut his legs off,
Cut them off at the knees,
He mounted his war horse,
And ran away across the road.
Damned him, the yellow Merchant,
He pushed his cut legs,
He pushed, to run without legs,
To get Marko the leader:
Three hours he chased him without legs,
Chased him across the white roads,
When he could not catch him,
From hardship he died!
If you could see Marko,
Marko then got praised,
For he was the champion of champions!

## Meaning

Again we see the role of the chthonic dragon being taken by a person, this time not by the black Arab but by the yellow Merchant. Marko and the yellow Merchant are the same individual, the ancestor and the child in whose body the ancestor will be reborn. The role of the midwife who instructs Marko how to be reborn here is taken by his own mother. She advises him how to kill his adversary and become the champion of champions.

The yellow Merchant is the ancestor, his heart of stone could represent the stone placed on the chest of the dead. The nine towers he built and the nine taps of the fountain represent the nine months of pregnancy. The towers, or a tower is simply an image of the womb, whereas a fountain is a symbol of the placenta. This is where Marko awaits disguised as a beggar, and I think that the symbolism and purpose of disguise is already understood by now. When the Merchant drinks from the ninth tap, when we are in the ninth month, the child is born and the umbilical cord is cut, represented as the cutting of the Merchant's legs. After three days (3 = time) of chasing, Marko wins (becomes immortal) – he is reborn.

## XII
## Marko Kraljević and the Arab

A bad dinner Marko dined:
Dry bread and cold water.
When he dined, he laughed,
So his old mother asked him:
„Oh my son, Kraljević Marko,
Do you laugh at the poor dinner,
Or at your mother,
For i have grown old, child?"
Thus spoke Kraljević Marko:
„Oh old woman, my old mother!
I don't laugh at the poor dinner,
God shall provide a better one,
Nor do I laugh at my old mother,
I too, a hero, shall grow old.
But it came to my mind, my mother!
When I was, mother, in captivity,
We were up to three hundred captives,
All in line we went for water,
My turn came, my mother!
They gave me a rusty saber,
And an old horse they gave me.
I took the jug and went to the water,
While going through the forest,
I wanted to unsheathe the saber

It didn't want to go out.

When I arrived at the water, in the forest,

The strong sun had burned me,

I grabbed, mother, the water,

And began washing my face with it,

Washing my face, and praying to God.

But rode a Turk Arab,

And asked a price for the water:

„Pay the tax, my unfortunate slave!"

And I asked him, mother,

How much is the price?

The Turk answered me:

„Either the head, or the right hand,

Or a hundred golden ducats."

So I answered him, mother:

„Away with you, Turk Arab!

I don't have enough,

To drink a bottle of wine!"

Unsheathed his saber the Turk Arab,

Hit me with it behind the neck,

Behind my neck burned a fierce fire.

And three times he hit me,

I grabbed my rusty saber,

I just touched it a little,

The saber came out by itself,

And I hit that Turk,

I struck him at his waist

As I hit him gently,

I cut him in two halves.
I took his garment,
Undressed it from him, put it on myself,
I took his horse and weapons,
And I took him to the tsar[16]
Asked me the tsar:
„By god, Kraljević Marko!
Why did you kill him?"
I answered the tsar, mother:
By God, my tsar!
If you did to me,
What the Turk Arab did,
I would cut your head as well!"
I began moving towards him,
The tsar moved away,
My heavy mace dragged behind me,
So when the tsar went over the bench,
And saw that he is in trouble,
Then spoke the tsar:
„Away you go Marko, from that devil!
I shall give you three chests of gold."
The tsar took out a hundred ducats,
And he gave the to me, mother!
Thus he said to me:
Here Marko, a hundred ducats,
Go drink wine in the tavern,
May my head be at peace!"

---

[16] To the Sultan, more precisely.

That came to my mind, my mother!
And that's why I laughed!"

## Meaning

I think that the meaning is obvious even to a child by now. Even though we don't have any symbolic numbers or elements in this song, when we compare it to the others it is clear that the Turk Arab is a substitute for the dragon, the ancient deity Veles, restraining the water and demanding a price for it. And this is why it was necessary to include this song and understand the Arab's role before we continue to the other song. However, I would like to firstly present you with a legend which is not very symbolic, but important because it contains traces of an ancient myth, and helps us understand Marko's role.

# XIII
## Marko's towers in Štip

I don't know when he lived. He made those towers, Marko's towers they are called, near the town Štip, up there on that peak. He aligned everyone from the river Bregalnitsa to carry stones, from one hand to another, and climb it up high. The workers worked, they finished everything. How long did it take them, that's their business, I don't know.

But his sister, she was very kind-hearted, and at that time she began to build the bridge above Bregalnitsa. She built a bridge, and Marko mocked her by saying:

- What are you building over there sister?

She said:

- Brother, I'm building a bridge so people can cross it for centuries. In your high towers owls will sing, but above my bridge the world shall pass!

He got angry and from above he threw a stone to kill her. He damaged the bridge a little bit. She ran away when she saw that he is throwing stones at her, to kill her. One stone fell on the hill, above the railway station, at a place called copper threshing floor. I don't know why it was called like that. When she arrived there, he threw a stone on the copper threshing floor. You can find the stone today, and there is still a handprint of Marko's fingers where he held it. The stone still stands there today.

**Meaning**

In this legend we don't find a lot of symbols, and the narrator doesn't know a lot of things either. However, the trained eye can easily recognize that this legend contains elements which stem from the deepest Proto-Slavic roots. In a way it resembles the battle of God and the Unclean one, of Saint Ilya and the Lamja, or more precisely of Perun and Veles/Vela. Firstly we have the classic division of space – Perun/ Marko is above, building towers on a peak, whereas his sister/Vela/Veles is below, near the water, building a bridge over the river. The original myth went through many changes and became a legend describing the relationship which Marko had with his sister, but the essence remained the same. Marko throwing stones at his sister from above, until he hits her or she hides undoubtedly reflects the primordial battle between Perun and Veles, in which Perun strikes Veles with weapons made of stone. Therefore we can easily conclude that Marko inherited the role of Perun in the South Slavic folklore, and that all the stones which Marko is said to have thrown, or walked upon and left his mark, originally belonged to Perun and the myths related to him.

Another element which confirms that this battle was indeed mythological is that the conflict ended when Marko threw the stone which can still be seen today in a place called "the copper threshing floor", and as I explained before, but also in detail in my first book "Chernobog's Riddles", the threshing floor made of copper, silver, gold, glass, crystal, or belonging to God, the fairies, and so forth, is *not* a real threshing floor, but a mythological space to which many myths and tales are linked. Essentially it is an image of the sky, the universe, the womb where we come from and return to. Since we have confirmed that Marko really did replace Perun we can proceed to examine some other mythological songs.

# XIV
# THE SISTER OF MARKO KRALJEVIĆ KILLS IN A DUEL IVAN OF SENJ

Ivan of Senj was showing off
In Senj, the white town:
„To all the girls of Senj
He has loved their faces,
But not the sister of Prince Marko.
He swore and promised,
That he will make love to her as well,
If nowhere, then on that cold water,
Early morning, or late in the night."
Ivan thought that nobody heard him,
But Kraljević Marko heard everything,
He was silent, as if he did not hear.
We went to his white courtyard,
In the courtyard he found his sister,
God's help he wished her:
„God's help, my dear sister,
Do not go to the cold water,
Early morning, or late in the night.

*(He continues to explain what happened, repeating verses 1 – 9.)*

The young maiden was silent, didn't speak a word
She went to the wardrobes,
Dressed the best she could,

She took an iron pitcher,
And walked to the cold water spring,
When she arrived at the water,
At the water was Ivan of Senj,
God's help she invoked:
„God's help, Ivan of Senj!"
„Be healthy, sister of Kraljević!"
So spoke Marko's sister:
„By God, Ivan of Senj,
Am I allowed to take water?"
You are, sister of Kraljević!
You are allowed, as much as you want."
When she filled the pitcher,
She sat down to rest,
To Ivan she spoke softly:
„By God, Ivan of Senj!
I have heard, but I have not seen,
That you have been showing off,
That to all the girls from Senj,
You have made love to,
Yet you have not loved me,
So you swore and promised,
That you will love my face,
If nowhere, on this cold water,
Early morning, or late in the night.
You won't, Ivan, I assure you!
If you don't believe me,
When the dawn dawns,

And the bright sun rises,
Dress the best you can,
We shall grab each other with our white hands,
We shall go to the wide field,
There I shall see you.
But if God and luck give me,
I will take a forged knife,
Slaughter you like a young lamb.
If you defeat me, Ivan,
Love, Ivan, my white face,
Love, Ivan, as much as you want."
When Ivan understood those words,
His heart danced with joy,
He could barely wait for dawn.
When the morning dawned,
And the bright sun rose,
They dressed the best they could,
Grabbed their white hands,
Walked to the flat field,
There they saw each other.
God and luck gave the maiden,
That she takes him,
And she took the forged knife,
She slaughtered him like a young lamb,
And she ran in her white courtyard,
Her old mother was joyful.

# Meaning

There is not much to be said about this song except that it is important to acknowledge the role Ivan has, and understand that he represents the dragon, ancestor, Veles, restraining the water and asking a price for it. However, the mythological elements in this song have been completely lost.

# XV
## THE SICK KRALJEVIĆ MARKO

Sick was Kraljević Marko,
Sick he was for nine years,
His whole family avoided him,
His beloved Angelina,
And his old mother,
Only his sister Anitsa remained,
To care for her brother's wounds,
So she spoke to her brother:
„Tell me, my dear brother,
Will you die, or heal?"
Oh Anitsa, my dear sister,
I won't die, I will be healed,
Only if I drink from the water,
From the spring which flows in the mountain."
„Your sister would go to the mountain,
But I fear Miyat the hajduk[17],
My first, brother, fiance."
„Go sister to my wardrobe,
Dress in my garment,
Which never in my life I wore,
Nor the sun has shined upon it."
She listened to her brother,

---

[17] In the Slavic South the hajduks were people who formed armed groups in the forests and fought against the Ottoman Turks.

She dressed like a Turk,
Wore the saber like a hajduk,
And she went in the mountain, to the water.
When in the mountain, at the water,
At the water was Miyat the hajduk:
„Where are you from, unknown hero?"
Where are you from, from which city?"
I'm the beloved of Vuk the fiery dragon,
The sister of Ljutica Bogdan."
Thus Miyat spoke to his company:
„Pour her cold water,
Escort her half way through the forest."
When half way through the forest,
Spoke the disguised maiden:
„Thank you, company of Miyat,
And Miyat, like my brother Marko,
I am not the beloved of the fiery Vuk,
Nor the sister of Ljutica Bogdan,
But the sister of Kraljević Marko,
Miyat's first fiancee."
Quickly the men went to Miyat,
Told their leader,
That the maiden whom water he gave,
Was not the love of the fiery Vuk,
Nor the sister of Ljutica Bogdan,
But the sister of Marko Kraljević,
Miyat's first fiancee,
And that the girl herself said that.

Jumped Miyat on his swift legs,

He saddled his black horse,

Until he was in the black forest,

The maiden went out of it,

Until he went out of the forest,

The maiden was in her courtyard,

Until Miyat was in the courtyard,

The maiden was in her brother's room.

Thus spoke Miyat the hajduk:

„Open the castle, Kraljević Marko,

Until now we were enemies,

From now on we shall be friends,

You will give me your dear sister,

To be my dearest fiancée."

The devil only knows what Marko answered.

## Meaning

Now in this version we can observe a symbolic pattern. Marko and his sister are the same individual who is going to be reborn. Marko's nine years of illness are the nine months of pregnancy, and he can not reincarnate unless he drinks from the water of the mountain. The water is of course the sacred spring under the tree, the fountain of youth, water of immortality, well of wisdom – the blood of the placenta; the ancestral honour. The hajduk is the dragon, the ancestor guarding the well in the underworld, this is why Marko's sister puts on a disguise, to enter the realm of the dead. In the previous song this is described as her dressing in the best clothes she has, but here we see that she dresses in a garment never worn before, and untouched by the sun – an obvious symbolism of the dead. Furthermore, it is said that she dresses like a

Turk, and we know by now what the Turks and Arabs replaced in these songs. She is allowed to fill water for her brother, Marko will drink it and will be healed he will be reborn, after the nine months of pregnancy, after drinking from the ancestral blood he will become whole. The words "heal", "whole" and "holy" have the same meaning. How the story continues only the devil knows, as the narrator said, but the possibility of the hajduk/ dragon being killed is always there.

# XVI
## Marko's sister deceived a champion at the well

Ill was Marko Kraljević,
Ill he was nine years,
The meat fell from his bones,
The sun shined through his bones,
Flies flied through his bones,
Avoided him his mother and beloved,
Only his sister Vangelina did not.
Marko spoke to his sister:
„By God, my dear sister!
You have done everything i said,
Do this, my dear sister!
Bring me water from the mountain,
To heal my wounds,
To make my horse happy."
„By God, my dear brother!
I did everything you said,
Yet I won't do this, my birth brother!
At the water is the great Yorlando,
Nine years he asked mother for my hand,
The tenth he asked you, dear brother,
You did not give me, nor promised me,
But you quarreled with him."
When her brother understood that,
To his sister he spoke:

„My dear sister!

Hear me, I will teach you.

Take these nine keys,

And go in the rooms above,

Put two white garments,

Nine rings on your fingers,

Each one is worth nine cities,

On your forehead put two precious stones,

With which you can dine,

And shoe nine horses,

At midnight like at midday,

On your head take an iron pitcher,

And go in the forest.

The great Yorlando will ask you,

Whose kin and of whose tribe you are,

And you answer, dear sister!

„I am the kin of Kraljević Marko,

From the tribe of Luka Senković,

Those are your good friends.

I was sent by Kraljević Marko,

To ask you for water from the mountain,

To heal his wounds,

To make his horse cheerful."

*(She does as instructed and takes the water. The tall Yorlando sent two servants to escort her back home.)*

When they arrived at the courtyard,
She searched in her pockets,
And spoke softly to the servants:
„Thank you for your company,
Here is for you a golden apple,
Which i have from my baptism day.
Give it to the great Yorlando,
May he love it, since he could not love me,
And tell him, dear followers,
That I am not the love of Kraljević Marko,
But his beautiful sister Vangelina."
Then she opened the gates,
And quickly closed them behind her.
She brought the water to her brother,
When Marko drank the water,
He thanked God,
And his only sister Vangelina,
So he jumped on his swift legs,
Like he was never ill,
He grabbed Šarac, his horse,
Jumped on his shoulders,
And rode through the green forest.
When home he returned,
Softly his sister told him:
„My dear brother,
I did everything you asked,
I went up to the water,
The great Yorlando sent his greetings,

And gladly gave you the water."
But hear, dear blood-brother!
What the great Yorlando did,
When his servants returned.
When to Yorlando they returned,
They told him softly:
„By God, our dear lord!
Here we are, we have returned,
And we carried out your order,
We filled a full pitcher of water,
Gently we put it on her head,
We escorted her to her courtyard.
Along the way she did not speak a word,
Yet before the white tower,
The young maiden told us:

*(They tell him what she said using the exact same verses, and they give him the golden apple.)*

When the tall Yorlando heard that,
He hit his knee with his hand,
As he hit so gently,
Three layers of clothes broke,
And a forth layer of skin and meat.
The precious stone, on his finger,
Broke in three parts,
Thus he weeped from his throat:
„Woe is me, my dear mother!

> I have not been deceived by a hero,
> But the beautiful sister of Kraljević."
> Then he gathered the adorned matchmakers,
> All the young, unmarried girls,
> All the young, unmarried boys,
> All good horses, never saddled,
> And went to ask the beautiful Vangelina,
> The beautiful sister of Kraljević.
> Marko saw them from afar,
> All of them playing guslas and tamburas,
> In front rode the great Yorlando,
> With a flag on a black horse…

To make a VERY long story short – Marko agrees to give his sister to Yorlando, but he asks of Yorlando to wait one week until his mother and sister return. When they do, they have a feast which lasts eight days, and on the ninth day Yorlando goes home with his bride. He marries Marko's sister after ten failed attempts.

## Meaning

Just as in the previous song here we find Marko being ill for nine years, but here the claim that he is the ancestor which is going to be reincarnated is strengthened by the way he appears in the verses i.e. literally as a skeleton. He of course will be reborn after he drinks from the water of the well which Yorlando keeps. Yorlando here is a giant, thus confirming once again that the giant in the South Slavic folklore has the same role as the dragon/ancestor/placenta – Veles. Marko's sister again puts on a disguise in order to be allowed to take from the water, and the nine months of pregnancy appear again as the nine rings she wears. She gives Yorlando a golden apple, which is always given when a maiden chooses her man, as we saw in the myth about the marriage of Jarilo and Mara. It is a symbol of immortality, rebirth, and enlightenment. Marko drinks from the water, from the blood of the placenta and he is reborn after nine years (months). However, the reincarnation is not over and will only be finished after the spirit is reunited with the ancestor i.e. when Marko's sister marries Yorlando.

Yorlando tried to marry Vangelina for ten times, which symbolizes the 10 lunar months of pregnancy. Yes, the pregnancy lasts nine solar months or ten lunar months. Then he needs to wait one week before Marko's mother and sister return. One week is seven days, this symbolizes the seven year old child who is about to go through the reincarnation ritual.

The ancestor will be reborn in his new body, that's what the marriage of the opposites represents. In the end we have a feast which ends on the ninth day, again a symbol of the nine months of pregnancy, thus completing the cycle of three pregnancies and successfully concluding the reincarnation ritual.

## XVII
## THE VILA THAT TOOK WATER TAX

Through the forest rode Kraljević Marko,
He rode, fiercely he cursed:
„May God kill you, black forest of mine,
When you don't have cold water,
For I am bored by my thirst.
I shall slaughter my horse,
To drink his blood!"
But the forest spoke to Marko:
„Don't curse, Marko, the black forest,
She is not to blame for anything,
But continue forward,
You shall find cold water.
On the water is the vila Mandolina,
She takes water tax:
From a horse, his rider,
From those who walk, their hand."
Marko did not worry,
He went forward,
Marko found the cold water,
But there was the vila Mandolina,
She had fallen asleep.
Quickly Marko drank water,
And his good horse drank as well,
Thus he stood and ran through the forest,
But woke the vila Mandalina,

And shouted to him:
„Hold, wait, unknown hero,
You have not paid the price!"
Then said Kraljević Marko:
„Come, fairy, so I pay your water!"
When the vila came to him,
Unsheathed Marko his saber,
Decapitated the vila Mandalina.

## Meaning

This song is very simple and it does not contain many symbolic elements. Here the figure which holds the waters captive and demands a price is not taken by a giant, Turk, Arab or Hajduk, but by a vila. The vila is an ancestral spirit, as previously concluded. She is the ancient chthonic Goddess of the underworld, the she – bear, the dragon who Marko needs to decapitate. The waters which she restrains represent the blood of the placenta, the life, honour, spirit of the ancestor which Marko, being the child, releases and drinks from. This is the same as the previously mentioned „immortal water" he drinks from. Naturally after the birth the umbilical cord is cut, and after the ritual reincarnation the ancestral skull is collected from the grave, represented here as the decapitation of the vila.

*Marko and the sleeping fairy*

## XVIII

## The Death of the Vila near the Lake

    Early rode Kraljević Marko,
On Šaran, his dueling horse,
Hunting in the forest he was.
He could not see any animals,
Let alone hunt anything,
A strong thirst conquered him,
To his horse he spoke:
„Oh Šaran, may the wolves eat you!
A strong thirst has come upon me!
I would even kill Šaran,
Drink the blood of Šaran,
Eat the meat of Šaran!
Heard him his sister in God,
Blood sister, the vila of the forest:
„Blood brother, Kraljević Marko!
Kill not the horse, waste do not make,
Drink not his blood, spoil not your soul
Eat not his meat, spoil not your body,
But ride the fairy horse Šaran.
When you arrive at the mountain peak,
You will find a dry fir,
And under the fir a green lake.
At the lake sits the vila,
Which demands a heavy price,

The arms of champions, up to the shoulder,

The legs of horses, up to the knees,

But she sleeps, may a snake bite her!

When Marko heard those words,

He rode his fairy horse,

Rode him up to the peak,

There he found the dry fir,

And the green lake underneath,

At the lake was a forest vila,

Which takes a high water tax,

The arms of champions, up to the shoulder,

The legs of horses, up to the knees.

There drank Kraljević Marko,

Drank he, and his horse,

And rode through the forest.

The devil didn't give him peace,

For he began to sing.

The vila woke from her sleep,

She grabbed a fast stag,

She bridled him with a fierce snake,

And rode after Marko quickly:

„Stop Marko, stop you bastard!

To pay for what you have done!"

Stopped Marko, took some ducats,

To pay for the water he drank.

Spoke to him the forest Vila:

„I do not need your ducats,

I want the arms to your shoulders,

And the horse's legs to his knees!"

Thus spoke Marko:

„You shall not have them, I swear!

Neither my arms,

Nor my horse's legs,

While my head stands on my shoulders!"

Thus he dismounted his Šaran

She dismounted as well,

Dismounted her fast stag,

And grabbed themselves by their chests.

They wrestled until midday,

Until Marko began to drool,

Drooled murky blood,

And the Vila's was as it was.

Marko became bored,

Thus he called upon his blood-sister,

Blood-sister, the Vila of the mountain:

„Today I am in trouble,

Don't you see, I'm almost dead!"

The Vila began to look,

From the right to the left,

How to help him against the other.

Marko threw her from right to left,

Hit the Vila on the ground,

Decapitated her, like a young lamb.

Marko was amazed to see,

The Vila had three heroic hearts:

One was calm, tired, dead,

The second was beating quickly,
On the third was a fierce snake,
Sleeping on it, may God kill her!
When Marko saw the snake,
He ran through the forest,
Back to Prilep, his town.
A long time ago it happened,
Yet we sing of it today.
We speak, to be joyful,
Make joyful, God, our kingdom!

## Meaning

In this song we see the same pattern as in the previous one, but with some more symbols to uncover. Marko is of course the foetus, and the seven year old child participating in the rencarnation ritual who will descend into the depths of the underworld. This is represented by the act of hunting, as the hunt always takes the hunter to the „other side", so to speak. That's a classic mytheme of many fairy tales and myths. Here we see that not only is there a lake where the vila is, but also a tree above it, representing the placenta and the tree growing above the bed of the dead. The water of the lake is the blood of the placenta, the honour of the dead (cf. The well of Mimir from which Odin drinks) whereas the sleeping vila is the ancestor (Veles, the dragon, the bear, cf. Mimir under Yggdrasil). The stag she rides bridled by a snake is another symbol of the placenta with the umbilical cord. But the stag's horns are also the tool to open the grave (womb), since in the stone age such antlers were used for digging up the graves of the dead.

After he decapitated the vila he saw that she has three hearts. The hearts represent the three pregnancy cycles, the symbolic heart placed on the chest of the dead, which the child collects when oppening up the grave. The third heart has a snake sleeping on it, and it also represents the umbilical cord, because before the cord is cut, it beats like a heart, along with the placenta. Normally Marko would kill the snake, as he killed the nine fierce snakes in the song called „Prince Marko & the Black Arab", when he split open the Arab. Nevertheless Marko in this song decides to flee, but that does not change anything in relation to the meaning of the song.

*The Fairy riding a stag*

~ 134 ~

# XIX
## The Vila of the Mountain

Through the forest rode Kraljević Marko,
Through the forest he rode, the forest he cursed:
„Oh damned black forest,
In you is not even a drop of water."
A hollow walnut tree was there,
In it a maiden yellow silk spun,
Thus she spoke to Kraljević Marko:
„Curse not the forest Prince Marko,
But ride forth a while,
You shall find a green lake,
It is guarded by a Vila,
Demanding a high price,
A hero's eyes from the head,
A horse's four legs."
Rode Marko forward a while,
Found he the green lake,
Drank he, and his horse as well,
But flew by, the tax demanding vila,
Thus she spoke to Kraljević Marko:
„You, pay the tax price!"
Marko Kraljević asked:
„How much will you take?"
„A hero's two eyes,
A horse's four legs!"

Thus spoke Marko:

„I shall give you silver uncounted!"

„I ask not for uncounted silver!

If uncounted silver I took,

I would fill the lake with silver!"

„I will buy you raw silk,

To cover the whole lake!"

„If raw silk I took,

The whole forest I would cover!"

They fought until midday,

Thus spoke Kraljević Marko:

„Vila, look up, is the sun high,

So I know at which time I die."

The vila looked up to see the sun,

Marko grabbed the saber from his waist,

Cut the head from her shoulders,

And said to it as she flew:

„Damn be, female head,

For fighting a hero in the forest!"

## Meaning

I don't think that an explanation for this song is needed. I trust that you can handle it on your own. I would just like to say that whenever we come across „midnight" or „midday" in the songs, tales and myths, we should think of the number twelve. The number twelve represents time, the full cycle of time and ultimately the winter solstice, when the final act of the reincarnation ritual takes place.

# XX
## Prince Marko and the Fairy Vida

Traveled Prince Marko,

Traveled across the forest green,

Hunting a fair stag.

Traveled he three days and nights,

Nowhere water did he find,

To cool his heroic throat,

No water to be found, no wine to be bought.

Cursed he the green forest:

„Oh, you forest, green forest!

May God allow that a fire burns you,

And in spring the frost covers you,

For not having a single drop of water,

To cool my heroic throat!

No water to find, no wine to buy!"

Spoke to him the fairy:

„Silence, Marko, dear blood-brother!

Curse not the green forest,

It's not her to blame,

Blame Vida the fairy,

Who locked twelve springs,

Amidst the forest, in a dry tree,

Dry all over, its peak is green!"

Marko first got angry,

Then he became ashamed,

He rode his fast horse,

The horse ran, searched, across the forest.

When he passed the whole forest,

He found that dry tree,

Dry all over, green at its peak.

He took his heavy mace,

Broke the tree apart,

Broke its twelve locks,

Burst the twelve springs!

Heard that the fairy Vida,

She grabbed a fair stag,

And three fierce snakes,

She bridled him with the two,

And used the third as a whip.

Quickly she caught Marko,

She jumped on his shoulders,

To take out his heroic eyes.

Marko begged her:

„Do not, sister, fairy Vida!

Take not my eyes!

If you want I shall pay the water,

If you want, with silver,

If you want, with gold!"

„Oh, you crazy Marko!

I need not your silver,

Nor do I need your gold,

I shall take your heroic eyes!"

Spoke to him the other fairy:

„Oh, Marko, dear blood – brother!

Why do you pray to that whore?
Why not pray to your heroic arms?"
Thus Marko grabbed her,
Grabbed her blonde hair,
He put her on his knees,
And pushed her with his mace,
So she begged him desperately:
„Gently, Marko, gently, brother
Gently strike with that heavy mace!"
„Oh Vida, you fairy whore!
My pleading you did not accept,
Why should I accept yours?"
Marko took out his saber,,
Cut her to pieces,
For his horse to see blood,
To see blood, to be pleased,
To be pleased and fly away,
Fly away up and high,
Up and high, across the blue sky!

## Meaning

In this song again we have to motif of the hunter being led to the „otherworld", „underworld" or the „cosmic axis", and he is led by nothing else than a fair stag. The stag is a prehistorical symbol which can be found all over Eurasia, and it usually appears in a hunting scene where the hunter by following it, leaves the ordinary world and arrives at a mythological place. In essence these myths and tales speak of a rebirth, for the person arrives to this netherworld and returns from it symbolically reborn.

We can trace back this motif to the prehistoric Neanderthal bear cult, for example in the burial of Le Regourdou, where the antlers of the stag were used to dig up the grave (in the netherworld, so to speak) of the dead, which is also one of the reasons why in the myths and tales the antlers of the stag are usually represented as golden. This also explains why the hunting scene is a very common motif on tombstones or burial goods, as the deceased was identified as the hunter (hero;deity) who went to the netherworld and will be reborn. The stag essentially represents the spirit of the ancestor leading the child to the grave – to himself, and it is his antlers with which the child will dig up the grave. In that sense, the child – Marko, and the stag are the same.

*South Slavic deer hunting scenes from tombstones*

When the songs speak, for example of traveling three days and nights, fighting three days, or eating and drinking three days, the meaning is always the same – the three pregnancies which fit within the annual cycle and end on the winter solstice. Therefore three is the time, and it bears a very close symbolical meaning to the number twelve.

Here we see that the fairy (the ancestor; the bear; the dragon; Vela / Veles) has locked twelve springs in a tree amidst the forest, and to give us a bigger hint that this tree is mythological, it is described as being „*dry all over, its peak is green*". It even resembles the ancient mistletoe, whose symbolism is the same.

The tree is of course the placenta and the tree growing above the burial mound, the water being held captive is the blood/life which Marko – the foetus, the child participating in the reincarnation ritual releases and drinks from. They are twelve, because as said before twelve is the time passed, the full cycle. The last month of the old year and the beginning of the new one, when on the winter solstice the final act of rebirth takes place. The snake bridled fairy stag was explained previously. Here Marko is again helped by his fairy blood-sister, his „good luck", his follower – the midwife who instructs him how to be reborn. As always, Marko decapitates the vila, even cuts her into pieces in this song. This is the cutting of the umbilical cord, the act of taking the ancestral skull.

Marko's horse is very pleased to see blood so he flies through the sky, but this is another metaphor. Marko's winged horse, or the Pegasus from the Hellenic myths always represents the placenta. The placenta glides out of the womb during childbirth as the flying horse glides through the air, towards the sky. When we remember that the sky is literally the womb, then these last verses simply describe the act of childbirth.

## XXI
## Marko and the Fairy Vela

Marko rode through the forest green,
Three days, water he did not find,
Thus he cursed the forest:
„Hey you forest, may you dry up,
Why don't you have a drop of water?"
And the forest said:
„Hey Marko I am not to blame,
The forest has nine wells!
May God kill Vela the vila,
Who took all nine wells,
Took them to a single place,
Closed them behind iron gates,
And placed upon them silver locks!
Turn your horse to the right side,
Where you shall see the tallest fir tree,
Whose top is made of gold!"
He turned his horse to the right,
And he found the tallest fir tree,
Whose top is made of gold!
He took out his mace,
Crushed the iron gates,
And unlocked the nine locks,
So he drank, and his horse as well.
„Let us ride my horse, and get away,

> For the fairy Vela shall see us,
> She will take your golden wings,
> And both of my black eyes!"
> Saw them she did, Vela the fairy,
> Took she the horse's golden wings,
> And Marko's two black eyes!

## Meaning

There we have it, as pure as it can be. Vela, the female appearance of Veles restricting the waters of the world in a tree, this time with a golden peak, behind nine locks. The tree is an obvious symbol of the cosmic axis, the placenta, with the nine wells being the nine months of pregnancy. Marko is Perun, the foetus, the one who wants to drink from the blood and be reborn. But unlike the other songs, this one tells of Marko's tragic fate, for the loss of his eyes represents his death. However, we have examined many songs before in which we have clearly seen that Marko defeats the fairy. Regardless of the outcome in this song, it is still important to acknowledge that the original name of the fairy restraining the waters in the tree of life is *Vela*. This can be confirmed by the fact that Vela appears as a Goddess, and a cognate of Veles in XIV century Russian sources. But also because she appears in the Baltic folklore[18] as *Velu mate* „mother of the dead", a synonym for *Kapa mate* „mother of the grave" and *Zemes mate* „mother earth".

This song *confirms* that the motifs which have been examined by now really are remnants of an ancient myth, describing the battle between Perun and Veles. And unlike the academic interpretation of these songs as being remnants of human sacrifice

---

[18] The mythology and folklore of the Baltic people is the closest to Slavic mythology and folklore. Even the languages are derived from a common Balto – Slavic root.

to the spirits of the water, I have confirmed here before you that such a claim is thoroughly *wrong*. In fact there is no evidence whatsoever to prove such a claim, whereas I have demonstrated through these songs that we are truly dealing with an ancient myth, which essentially describes the process of reincarnation.

If you still doubt that the Ala/Lamja/Aždaja essentially represented Vela/Veles, and that Marko is the successor of Perun, I invite you to read the following song.

# XXII

## Marko and the three headed Ala

Further evidence that Vela, or Veles (Triglav) is really behind the dragon, known as Ala, Lamja or Aždaja, lies in the verses of the following song, where Vela is replaced by a three headed Ala in the exact same context as the previous song:

> Three days Marko rode through the forest,
> Three days traveled, searched for water,
> There was no water in the forest,
> There were no springs near the roads.
> Marko cursed the forest:
> „Damn you, forest!
> For you do not have a single spring,
> And you don't have springs near the road,
> For a traveler to drink,
> For his horse to drink."
> Thus the forest spoke in sorrow:
> „I have springs in the forest,
> The Ala has restrained them,
> Does not allow a man to pass,
> To pass, to drink water,
> To pass, to let his horse drink.
> You go over two, over three peaks,
> Find the large springs,
> Which the Ala restrained!"
> Marko went and his horse drank,
> The three headed Ala saw him,

> With three heads and nine tongues,
> Thus spoke to Marko:
> „Oh Marko, unknown hero!
> How could you drink water?
> How could you let your horse drink?"
> Marko thus answered:
> „How much does the water cost?
> If it costs, I shall pay with groschen,
> If it costs, I shall pay with gold.
> Thus the Ala spoke:
> „If I took groschen, the whole mountain would be silver,
> If I took gold, the whole forest would be golden,
> But tell me, unknown hero,
> Should I kill you young,
> Or take your horse's eyes?"

As you can see the context of this song is identical to the previous one, with slight differences but same essential symbolism. Here there aren't nine wells, but the Ala taking the role of Triglav – Veles has nine tongues. Regardless of the variations, the meaning remains the same, and I'm sure you know what happened to the Ala after she asked Marko that question. There can not be any more doubt regarding who these songs are essentially about and what they essentially represent. Now let's go forth and find an unexpected evolution of the symbols.

*Marko & the Three Headed Dragon*

# XXIII

## Mara gives wine and food to Marko Kraljević, but not to the Turks

Marko traveled across the whole land,

Three days he traveled, water he did not find,

He wanted to kill his horse,

To drink his black blood.

His horse spoke to him:

„Don't, Marko, do not kill me,

But move a bit further,

You will find two beautiful firs,

Beneath them two cold wells,

The firs are guarded within a fort.

Amidst the courtyard is a cool tavern,

Within walks the young tavern maiden,

She will, Marko, open the gates!

Listened Marko to his horse,

Moved he further up,

Found he the two beautiful firs,

And saw the fort built around,

With its closed gates.

When Marko came at the gates,

Knocked he on the gates,

And three times he shouted:

„Open up, young tavern maiden,

Open or I shall die for a glass,

Three days I travel, water I do not find!"

Arrived the young tavern maiden,

And opened the gates,
With right hand she greeted Marko,
She took his horse with the left,
And welcomed them in,
Thus she spoke to Marko:
„Praised be, unknown hero,
For you there is a roasted lamb,
For you there is wine, three years old,
For the horse there is white hay!"
So Marko sat in the tavern,
To eat a roasted lamb,
And drink wine three years old,
And he asked the maiden:
„Why are you alone in the tavern,
Are you a maiden, or a bride?"
She answered him silently:
„Oh you, unknown hero,
I am not a maiden, nor a bride.
I married as a young tavern maiden,
Three weeks did not pass,
The Arnaut[19] Turks came
And took my first love away.
It has been nine years,
As I wait for my love to return,
Which is why I opened the gates for you.
When I hear Bulgarian voices,

---

[19] Arnaut is a Turkish ethnonym used to denote Albanians, derived from the Greek Ἀρβανίτης "Árbanítis", which is a later variation of Ἀλβανίτης "Álbanítis".

I open up quickly,
But when I hear Turkish voices,
I quickly run and hide!"
Just as she said those words,
Her love opened the gates,
Marko he hugged,
And kissed his feet.

## Meaning

Well I think that we can all agree that the ending is a bit weird. Marko literally did not do anything, but he is being hugged and has his feet kissed by a man who just arrived home after being held nine years in captivity. Despite this little funny ending, the song is important to understand how the symbols evolved in the folklore. It begins like all the previous ones, with Marko being thirsty and searching for water, however, the womb, the cosmic axis, the „underworld" now is not just represented as the wells under the trees, but also by a tavern.

A tavern is of course the place where Marko drinks wine, an avatar of the blood feeding the foetus. Therefore, whenever we encounter the tavern from now on we should understand it as such. Another thing which also points to the fact that the place Marko goes to, being indeed the womb/burial mound, is that it is guarded by the walls of a fortress. It is inaccessible to the Turks, but it is to Marko, naturally since he is about to be reborn. There Marko finds a tavern maiden who has been waiting for her beloved for nine years, representing the nine months of pregnancy. Marko and her beloved are essentially the same, whilst she and Marko/her beloved are the same individual split in two because of the mythological context.

The reunion of the opposites, the spirit of the ancestor and the child, represents the final act of rebirth. Therefore, Marko goes to the tavern/womb/burial mound where he eats and drinks wine – the avatar of blood. After nine years the maiden's love returns, representing the nine months of pregnancy and the reunion of the spirit with his new body. Marko is reborn.

## XXIV
## Kraljević Marko Avenges His Brother's Death

Through the forest rode Kraljević Marko,

With him rode his brother Andrijaš,

Andrijaš was seven years old,

But it was not a very strong child,

He became very thirsty,

Thus he spoke to his brother:

„Oh, brother of mine, Kraljević Marko!

Is there a cold water well somewhere,

To drink some water from it?"

Marko answered him:

„By God, brother Andrijaš,

There is no well of cold water,

But let's ride forth through the forest,

In the forest is Mara the tavern maiden,

Who pours wine and rakija."

When they arrived to the white tavern,

Spoke Marko to his brother:

„Oh by God, brother Andrijaš!

Go now to the tavern maiden Mara,

But in the tavern there are always Turks,

Be careful, they might take your head!"

But Andrijaš was weak,

When he rode to the tavern,

Came out the tavern maiden Mara:

Made him smile with her white teeth,
Seduced him with her black eyes,
Asked him for the horse and weapons,
He gave her the horse and weapons.
Entered the hero in the tavern,
In the tavern were thirty Turks,
Drinking red wine.
They greeted him with a cup of wine,
Andrijaš drank all the cups,
For the hero was very thirsty,
Quickly he got drunk from the wine,
Fell Andrijaš with his head on the table.
When the Turks saw that,
That Andrijaš got quickly drunk,
They grabbed their sharp sabers,
Cut off the head of Andrijaš,
Placed on the table.
Whenever a cup of wine arrived for him,
They poured it on his dead head.
Waited for him his brother Marko,
Waited until midday, on a summer's day.
He could not wait any longer,
So he went to search for him,
He rode to Mara the tavern maiden.
When he arrived at the tavern,
Mara went out to meet him,
With her white teeth she made him smile,
Seduced him with her black eyes,

Asked him for the horse and weapons,

He slapped her face with his hand,

He slapped her so gently,

Knocked out two white teeth from her,

Three bloody wounds burst to bleed.

Thus he went in the tavern.

When the hero entered the tavern,

Thirty Turks drank wine,

He recognized his brother's head.

All the Turks greeted him with a cup,

The hero Marko did not look at the cups,

Unsheathed he his saber sharp,

And decapitated all the Turks,

Not one did he let live,

Except one, Skenderbeg Mujo.

He buried his brother,

And adorned his grave with Turkish heads,

Thus he sang loudly:

„Thanks and praises to the dear God!

For I have avenged my brother Andrijaš!

Who shall avenge me?

Mother I do not have, nor a sister,

In my kin, I have none."

# Meaning

Personally I love how these songs have developed. Several versions of this song exist and they vary in little insignificant details, yet in essence they have preserved so much of the ancient reincarnation tradition. Honestly, if we did not know that the children at the age of seven descended in the burial mounds of their ancestors and collected their skulls, this song would make no sense. And we would be left to wonder why a seven year old child would go get drunk in a tavern full of Turks, whilst the official „authorities" would provide us with vague and obscure explanations, if they even cared to examine these songs at all.

Marko and his brother are the same individual split in two, in the same way that the hero and the princess of classic tales are. He is the double of Marko, acting as the ancestor who needs to die in order for Marko to live i.e. to be reborn. Like in the previous songs, they ride through the forest and Andrijaš is taken over by thirst, so he descends into the realm of the dead, to the lake of the vila from the previous songs, or Mara's tavern. Mara is also the name of the Slavic Goddess of winter and death whose effigy is burned every spring equinox, marking the death and rebirth of nature. So we are possibly dealing with a mythological layer where Mara, as Vela, rules over the realm of the dead, which would not be a surprise since her very name is derived from the PIE root *mar-, *mor- meaning death. Just as Vela, she is the she bear, the mother of the dead who allows the participants of the ritual to enter the underworld – the tavern. Andrijaš there gets drunk with thirty Turks, and we know from the previous songs that the Turks and Arabs are the successors of the ancient dragons. Therefore the thirty Turks are nothing else than the three headed dragon – Triglav/Veles. The decapitated head of Andrijaš is the head which the child participating in the reincarnation ritual (Marko; Perun; Jarilo) collects from the grave, representing his successful rebirth.

The reincarnation of his psyche in the new body of the seven year old child. Marko (the child) descends into the underworld, the tavern, to save his brother from the thirty Turks – the three headed dragon. He decapitates the Turks and collects the head of his brother – the ancestor. Marko is successfully reincarnated.

# XXV

## THE DEATH OF KRALJEVIĆ MARKO

Well we have been through the songs and tales describing Marko's birth, marriage, heroic battles and many other adventures, so now all that remains is to see how Marko died. Marko's death can appear differently. Sometimes he dies from sickness, because he is too wounded and can not be healed, or even simply because it was his time to go. Most songs describing his death say that he was buried in the Hilandar monastery.

We already saw that there are legends which say that Marko became immortal because he drank from the water of the fairies, the eagle water, or simply the immortal water, and that he lives in heaven with Saint Ilya. And it is true, Marko did drink from that water, the water which made him immortal i.e. which enabled his rebirth, as we have seen in many examples so far. Therefore Marko can not really die, which is why the majority of the songs and tales say that Marko continued to live in a cave, or some distant land, from where he will return and bring order on earth once more. The meaning of all the tales and songs which deal with this motif will be explained in the end.

**The tale begins:**

One morning Marko's blood-sister, the vila Zagorkinja, told him that he has lived enough, 365 years, and that he will die within three days. Then Marko went to a large cave and from there he threw his mace into the sea, saying „When this mace comes out of the sea, then the Turks will go back over the sea!" He then placed a large stalk of hay for his horse to eat, saying „When Šarac eats this hay, I shall wake up!" Finally, he struck his saber into a stone and said „When this saber comes out of the stone, the Serbian people shall have their empire back!" After this Marko went in the cave and fell asleep. It is said that the mace is almost out of the water, that the horse will finish eating the hay soon, and that the saber is halfway out of the stone.

## XXVI
## King Marko and the firearm

Once while Marko lived on this land, when he fought the Turks, defended the land and dealt justice, the firearm appeared. When it appeared, a boy took a pistol and told Marko „Oh, king Marko, your time has come as well, to not exist anymore as heroes!" Marko asked him why, to which the boy replied „Well here, I can kill you with this!" „What is that?" Marko asked, and the boy answered „It's called a pistol." Marko held out his right hand and the child shot it, so Marko was amazed. „It's so little! There is no life for us here anymore!" So he went in a cave, he hanged his saber, he struck the saber in a stone, he removed the saddle from his horse and said „When the saber will go out of the stone, and the saddle will be back on the horse, I shall come out of the cave and rule the land again!"

# XXVII
## King Marko is alive

Once during the Bulgarian war, a soldier from Prilep was a soldier on the Black Sea. The army there had little boats with which the soldiers patrolled the sea. The soldier from Prilep went in the boat, and when a strong wind blew, it took him across the sea. The man held on, he did not know where he was, and soon night fell over the stormy sea. Eventually the wind stopped and the man saw a cliff amidst the sea, like an island. He went with the boat to the cliff and there he found a cave, so he looked inside and saw a large man with a big head who was sitting. He came to the entrance, but he was afraid to go in, so the man from inside said „Come in, what are you afraid of?" When the soldier understood that the man spoke his language, he thought that he could reason with him, so he went in and said „Good evening!" and the man replied „Good evening! Sit!" He sat and the man asked him „Why are you afraid?" so the soldier explained to him what happened, and that he does not know how to return. „Don't be afraid!" - the man said - „You will return where you came from. Where are you from?" „From Prilep." replied the soldier. „And have you heard anything in Prilep about Kraljević Marko?" asked the large man. "Yes, I have. There are statues of him there, the ruins of his old castle and his towers. The children learn about him when they study history." Then the man replied "I am Kraljević Marko, and I was born there, in Prilep!" So the soldier asked Marko „Why do you not come and live there among us?" To which Marko replied „As long as there is firearm, I am not coming out of this cave. I shall return when no such weapons exist anymore!" The soldier said „But the weapons are becoming more and more modern, constantly improving!" So Marko replied „Yes, but the modern weapon is like the wind which brought you here, one day it will be no more. There will be no modern weapons! Now listen, go to sleep and tomorrow you will be at the place where you were. What you heard and saw you will say. I am alive, and one day I shall return!"

So the soldier fell asleep, and when he woke up he was in his boat, on the harbour of the army, but he did not know how he got there. He went to the army and they were surprised to see him, for they thought he was dead. Some time later they released him from the army and he went back to Prilep, telling everyone around that he met King Marko, and that he will one day return again.

*King Marko, the king under the mountain*

## XXVIII
## Marko Kraljević is not dead

A man rode through the forest to a place where he could buy wine for his name day celebration. Ho bought two barrels, put them on his horse and rode back. But tasting the wine and negotiating the price took him too much time, the night fell when he was returning home. He took the wrong road, got lost and arrived in front of a cave, not knowing how to return. He went in the cave because he wanted to spend the night under shelter, and noticed that the cave was very deep, and within its depths a fire was burning. He was curious to know who lit the fire in the cave, so he went deeper and slowly made his way by the stone walls. Suddenly a white lady appeared before him, whose magical glow covered her whole body. The man recognized a fairy, he got frightened, almost fell even, but the fairy (vila) told him not to be afraid, for she is not an enemy of good folk. He explained to her his trouble and how he arrived to the cave, and asked her if he can spend the night there. She allowed him, so he removed the weight from his horse and she showed him the way to the fire. He wanted to know what was keeping the fairy in the cave, so she told him that her blood-brother, Kraljević Marko, lives there and that she is guarding him. The man's heart danced with joy, and he wished to see the glorious hero with his own eyes, for he had heard many songs and tales about him. So he asked the fairy if it was possible to see him, even just for a moment.

She told him to follow her, and an iron door opened before them behind which stood Šarac, Marko's loyal horse. The fairy touched him gently and he moved out of the way. Thus before the man's eyes appeared a tall and wide hall, and amidst it hanged a damascus saber, with colourful reflections from the precious stones on its handle illuminating the hall. Beneath the saber sat Kraljević Marko on a stone throne and a stone table in front of him. The hero's hair and beard were long and white, as if covered by snow from the mountain, and his eyes were dead and blind.

He stood up and asked the fairy „I hear a man, who is it?" The fairy explained what happened to the stranger, and that she allowed him to spend the night in the cave. Marko listened to the fairy's words, and spoke to the man „Come, step forth brother, let's kiss, and shake my hand so i can see how strong the people of these times are!" Joyfully the man went towards Marko, but the fairy stopped him, saying that he should be careful if his life was dear, for the hero's embrace could shake off his head, and his fist could break his bones. So in one hand she gave him a mighty iron bar which was heated up from the fire, and in the other hand she gave him a mighty iron pumpkin. The man went towards Marko with the bright iron bar, Marko grabbed it and squeezed it so hard that water dripped from it. The man then gave him the iron pumpkin, and Marko grabbed it so tight that he left his hand print on it and said „Oh, how weak the men have become today!"

The man said „Marko, many songs and tales say that you died many years ago." Marko answered him „I have not died, brother, I wait for my time to come again when I will go out and rid the world from all evil and injustce!" The man asked when will that time come, and Marko replied „Look at the saber which hangs above my head! I can not see it, but I feel its bright reflection. When the world will be full of evil and injustice, it will unsheathe by itself and come to my hands. See for yourself! The time is coming! The saber is almost completely out! Then I shall ride my loyal horse, God shall give me my eyes back, and i shall strike at the evil and unjust, to give to everyone what they deserve! It will be a bloody battle – might shall break might! After the bloody victory again I shall return to this cave, on this hard throne. A stone ties him to the earth, no human power shall replace me. Above my head I shall hang my saber, underneath it shall be my golden cup, the blood of the saber shall drip in the cup and I shall drink it when it's full. The last cup I drink will be filled with the last blood, which my strength shall spill on this land. By God's will, there will be no need for Kraljević Marko afterwards." Marko got lost in his thoughts, in his mind he heard the ringing of the clashing swords, and the screaming of the battle horses. He came back to himself, the battle sounds went silent, and Marko asked the man „How much do you charge for the wine? Fill my cup so I can taste it! I have not drank wine in 300 years." The man gladly brought him a barrel, Marko drank it in one sip and asked for another one. The man gave him the other barrel, Marko drank it quickly and asked the man how much wine he drank, to which the man replied „Two barrels!" Thus Marko said „Oh, sad world, what have you become, what a scam for two barrels! What was in the past two cups has become two barrels!"

He told the fairy to give the man some money so he could buy more wine for his celebration, and he ordered the man not to speak to anyone of what he saw and what he heard, until his death. And so it was.

## XXIX
## Marko in the Cave

Cut the Turk the green field,
In Kunar the high mountain,
His name was Džidovina Meo.
How the Turk worked quickly,
With the scythe moving in the distance,
When the time came to rest,
Lied the Turk in a soft shade,
As he lied, so he fell asleep.
In his sleep he had a strange dream,
That it was not his field, but a fairy cave,
In the cave was a great man,
Terrifying as a cloud,
On him raw bear skin,
His hat of wolf skin,
As he snores the cave echoes,
Over his lap he holds a saber,
Which unsheathes by itself,
As if it craves a battle and duel,
Male blood and the enemies wounds.
Saw the Turk that he stumbled upon,
The champion Kraljević Marko,
And thought to himself,
That he will not see a white day again.
So the Turk rolled his eyes,

And beheld another terrifying thing,
Marko's dueling horse, Šarac,
Eating moss with his teeth.
In front of Marko sat the vila Ravijola,
Holding a gusla of maple wood,
The gusla played by itself,
And sang of Serbian glory,
Marko drinks wine from a bowl,
Served by the fairy Ravijola,
A bowl of twelve okas.[20]
Thus spoke Kraljević Marko:
„Farewell, Džidovana Meo,
Greet my Serbian brothers,
May they renounce the miserable firearm,
With which they ruined their own houses,
Until I return, a hero among Serbs,
With my battle horse Šarac,
Then heaven shall return again!"

## Meaning

The motif of the king sleeping under the mountain is a very old one and it can be found all over Europe, but similar motifs can also be found across Asia and the Americas. Some examples of such kings or heroes are King Arthur, Frederick Barbarossa, Ogier the Dane, Charlemagne, whereas in Slavic lands other such figures besides Kraljević Marko are Matija Gubec, Kralj Matijaž, Wenceslas I, and so forth.

---

[20] The oka was an Ottoman measure of mass.

The motif is pre-Christian, but was such an important one that it survived the Christianization of Europe, and replaced the ancient deities and heroes with Kings, or more recent heroes. However, the context did not change, and the meaning of the tales remained the same – reincarnation.

These tales are always the same, with slight differences and usually only the names of the kings replaced. The cave within which Marko resides is the burial mound, the grave, the womb, and he is the ancestor which is going to be reborn, when his time comes. This is why he is always represented with very long white hair and beard, but also being blind, which is a symbolic way to represent one's death. However, within the tales his time to be reborn hasn't come yet, .He is immortal, because he is the sum of the ancestors, the essence of the psyche which is immortal and timeless, thus he is sleeping in the cave only to return again and fight, until his time comes to go back in the cave, and so the cycle continues. This is the metaphor of life, death and rebirth. We are born, we fight through life, we die, and we are born again to fight again. This is in essence the exact same myth as the Norse one about Valhalla, Odin's hall of the fallen, or rather hall of the chosen. Yes, those chosen to be reborn, as explained in the book „Paganism Explained, Part IV: Valholl & Odinn in Yggdrasil".

In the first tale before Marko enters the cave he throws his mace in the sea, and struck his saber into a stone, saying that when they come out he will return again, banish the Turks across the sea and bring back the Serbian Empire. The sea where Marko throws his mace is a symbol of the underworld, of death and the burial mound. His mace is the weapon of the thunderer, which as previously explained is a metaphor for the heart of the dead – Life itself. The biface placed on the chest of the dead by the Neanderthals. Just as Thor retrieves his hammer and is thus reborn, or Zeus retrieves his thunderbolts, so Marko will have his mace when he returns back to life i.e. he will rekindle the fire of his heart, and defeat the Turks (remember that the Turk is the dragon – ancestor). The saber which Marko struck in the stone is an identical symbol as the Arthurian sword Excalibur which could only be taken out of the stone by Arthur, the one destined to be the king of Britain. Therefore, just as Arthur pulls the sword out of the stone and becomes king i.e. is reborn, so Marko will be reborn when his saber falls out of the stone, or completely unsheathes, for it is the same symbolism, as shown in the tale „Marko and Philip the Magyar". The sword or saber stuck in the stone is a symbol of the umbilical cord attached to the placenta, and naturally when a child is born the umbilical cord is cut. The sword is unsheathed, or removed from the stone.

Furthermore, Marko is described as wearing raw bear skin, whose symbolism has been previously explained, but here we find another link to king Arthur, whose name literally means „bear". He, just as Marko, is the ancestor chosen to be reborn.

Marko's winged horse is also the placenta, naturally present with him in the cave – womb. We already saw that the horse glides through the air just as the placenta glides out of the womb, carrying Marko – the foetus. The horse represents the placenta in all mythologies, especially winged horses like that of Marko, or Pegasus, but also Odin's horse Sleipnir whose name literally means „the glider". A white horse was the animal which was kept in the temple of the Slavic God Sventovit on the isle of Rugen. Sventovit, whose name means „imbued with divine power", is a much later name and a local variation of Perun, who as we have seen in many examples was the predecessor of King Marko. We don't know if his horse was also represented with wings, but I would say it probably was. Nevertheless, the historical sources inform us that the Slavs of Rugen reported having seen a few times the horse dirty, sweaty and tired in the morning, because Sventovit was riding it all night, fighting against the enemies of the people. This is of course just another metaphor, telling us that each morning Sventovit is reborn, for he fought the enemies during the night i.e. during death.

The link between death and night in Slavic traditions is confirmed by the many folk accounts which regard sleep as „small death", and the dreams as messages from the ancestors, fairies, saints, God, or in the distant past, from the Gods. They regarded dreaming as a journey to the „other side" where one could meet certain mythological or ancestral figures which would instruct the dreamer what to do in his life. So for example in the song „Marko in the cave" we see that the person encounters Marko in his dream, and not physically. Or in the tale where the soldier is drifted away to Marko's cave, he returns from there by ... waking up. And Marko's cave is located on an island amidst the sea, which is the best way to represent the womb, the cosmic axis, which is identical to the „centre" of the psyche – the sacred space of healing, regeneration and rebirth.

As always, Marko is represented as drinking wine, in the last song he drinks wine from a bowl of twelve okas. The number twelve represents the twelve months of the year, the time passed before the act of reincarnation. In another tale Marko not only drinks wine, but also the blood of his enemies which drips from his saber. His enemies are of course the ancestors which he overcomes, or rather becomes, by drinking their blood from the saber. An excellent way to represent the blood of the umbilical cord nourishing the foetus in the womb, until it „leaves the cave and rids the world of all evil and injustice".

Sventovit apparently also drank wine. In the description of Sventovit from Rugen, his idol was represented holding a large drinking horn made of various metals. Once per year the horn was filled with new wine which would last until the next year. Depending on how much the wine disappeared during the year, the sorcerer responsible for the temple concluded whether or not the next year would be bountiful or not.

Marko's abandonment of the world due to the appearance of firearms is simply because there is no honour in a battle with firearms, for it is no longer the might and the skill of men which wins the battle, but technology. With modern weapons anyone can be a „hero", even a little boy. Marko foresaw the downfall of man due to technology replacing most of his abilities, and decided to withdraw himself from it. And he was right, our technological progress has deprived us from most of our natural abilities, but when this civilization falls, as all other before, the sleeping king shall awaken and bring order to the world once again.

# Epilogue

On the journey through the Serbian and South Slavic epic poetry, fairy tales and legends, we were able to meet Kraljević Marko, the most famous hero and king of the land. We learned about his birth, life, struggles, adventures and his symbolical death.

Along the journey we understood, through many examples, that these mythological motifs in which Marko appears are remnants of more ancient myths, and which stem from the deepest pre-historic Neanderthal past. Although we can not be sure that the common folk of the Balkans still understood the meaning of the symbols, or just preserved the tradition simply because its role : tradition; it makes no difference to us. We have removed the many Christian and Ottoman layers of the songs and tales, and what remained in the end was their pure pagan essence.

The essence which speaks of the rebirth of the Gods, the reincarnation of the divine in a new body, described in the songs as none other than Marko. The great champion inherited the role of the ancient Slavic thunder god Perun, for we have seen and confirmed that most of the songs speak of battle with his adversary, Veles. In a dominantly Christian era, the only way to preserve the ancient knowledge was to transmit it in a modified form, with kings, heroes and fairies replacing the ancient Gods. Later on when people got under Ottoman threat, it was none other than Kraljević Marko, the ancient god, who took on the role of protector for the same reason. The myths which preceded the historical Marko Mrnjavčević still represented the core of the people.

Marko thus became what once was a divinity. He became the indestructible, immovable and timeless essence of each individual which is constantly reborn in the kin, as the songs and tales speak. He became the sum of the people, their ancestors and ancient traditions.

However, Marko's adversary sometimes appears as a seven year old child, which is very confusing when we know that nobody was a match for his power. Well, I am happy to say that the riddle which has bothered many for so long has finally been solved. The secrets of the past have been highlighted, and we can continue to walk our ancestral path with honour and pride.

Marko is Perun, the essence and sum of the kin which is always reborn. This rebirth can be biological, through the womb of the mother, but also spiritual, through the descend into the underworld, obtaining the name of the honourable dead – yourself. Marko is thus the foetus in the womb and the child at the age of seven participating in the reincarnation ritual. He takes the head of Veles, the dragon, the ancestor, and is therefore reborn. Himself given to himself.

Therefore, this is why the guslar, the sorcerer played these songs for the people. He invoked the divine in the people's psyche and thus helped them realize, or rather remember, that the songs played and sang are essentially about them. They are Marko, i.e. the Gods, they are immortal. As you could see in the past, the concept of God or the divine was completely different than what our mindset is today, thanks to the Abrahamic religions. The divine was not supernatural, it was not above and beyond nature, but in the very infinitude of nature, the cosmos and in man. The divine can not be considered beyond nature, for nature is divine itself. It is timeless and eternal. It simply *is*. What is considered as supernatural in our traditions, was for our ancestors like a veil hiding the truth of divine fortitude.

Gods are like shadows moving on the wall of Plato's cave, and those who did not understand the nature of the divine believed the shadows to be the truth. Like a child believing in Santa Claus. However, those who turned around and left the cave understood the true nature of the divine, for they were elevated to it, and embodied it. They became the Gods themselves. This was the purpose of the guslar who sang the ancient myths, and later on the epic songs of Marko. As a midwife of the mind he helped people exit the cave to finally see the truth. I am honoured to have written this book , which will, hopefully bring you a clear understanding. If you do, then I congratulate you for finally seeing the light.

# BIBLIOGRAPHY

Краљевић Марко, народна песмарица, Београд : Државна штампарија Краљевине Србије, 1913., стр. 1-2

Трем на българската народна историческа епика. От Момчила и Крали Марка до Караджата и Хаджи Димитра. Съст. Божан Ангелов и Христо Вакарелски. София, 1939

Др. Војислав С. Радовановић: Маријовци у песми, причи и шали, Штампарија Василија Димитријевића Скопје, 1932.

Сборник за народни умотворения и народопис : Книга 44 (1949) Народни песни и приказки от Софийско и Ботевградско / Георги Поп Иванов; Под редакцията на проф. Ст.Романски, стр. 23-25.

Сборник от български народни умотворения. Част I. Простонародна българска поезия или български народни песни (Отдел I и II. Самовилски, религиозни и обредни песни. Книга I). София, 1891

Виенац уздарја народнога о Андији Качић-Миошићу на столиетни дан преминутја, 1861. у Задру, стр. 140-141.

Хрватске народне пјесме, скупила и издала Матица хрватска. Одио први. Јуначке пјесме. Загреб 1890-1940.

Български народни песни от Македония. Събрал Панчо Михайлов. София, 1924.

Др. Војислав С. Радовановић: Маријовци у песми, причи и шали, Штампарија Василија Димитријевића Скопје, 1932.

Olinko Delorko: Narodne pjesme otoka Zlarina, "Narodna umjetnost", 1980, knjiga 17, str. 300-301.

Геземан, Г. (1925). Ерлангенски рукопис старих српскохрватских народних песама. Сремски Карловци: СКА.

Srpske narodne pjesme iz zbirke Novice Šaulića; Grafički institut "Narodna misao", Beograd – 1929

Хрватске народне пјесме, сакупљене страном по приморју а страном по граници, сабрао Стјепан Мажуранић, учитељ, свезак I, у Сењу, тиском и накладом Х. Лустера, 1876., стр. 28-30.

Хрватске народне пјесме, што се пјевају у Горњој хрватској Крајини и у турској Хрватској; сабрао Лука Марјановић; Свезак I, у Загребу 1864

Александар Лома - "Пракосово: словенски и индоевропски корени српске епике", Балканолошки институт САНУ, Београд, 2002

Слободан Зечевић - „Митска бића српских предања", Вук Караџић, Београд, 1981

Radoslav Katičić – „Božanski boj", Ibis grafika, Zagreb, 2008

*Studia Mithologica Slavica, 10, 2007, pp. 83-104.*

Чаусидис, Никос - Митологизираното гумно во словснската традиционална култура - I

Веселин Чајкановић - „Мит и религија у Срба", СКЗ, Београд, 1973

Ш. Кулишић, П. Ж Петровић, Н Пантелић - "Српски митолошки речник", Нолит, Београд, 1970

В.В. Иванов, В.Н.Топоров - "Исследования в области славянских древностей", Наука, Москва, 1974

Cachet, Marie, "The Secret of the She-Bear : An Unexpected Key to Understand European Mythologies, Traditions and Tales", Createspace, 2017

Vikernes, Varg, Cachet, Marie "Paganism Explained" ( Series I – V), Create Space, 2017 - 2019

Luka Trkanjec – „Chthonic aspects of the Pomeranian deity Triglav and other tricephalic characters in Slavic mythology", SMS XVI, 13, str. 9-25.

Slavische Volkforschungen, Abhandlungen über Glauben, Gewohnheitrechte, Sitten, Bräuche und die Guslarenlieder der Südslaven Vorwiegend auf Grund eigener Erhebungen Von Dr. Friedrich S. Krauss., Verlag von Wilhelm Heims, Leipzig 1908

Neroznak, V. Paleo-Balkan Languages. Moscow, 1978

Manufactured by Amazon.ca
Bolton, ON

29896647R00101